Bryan Adams:
A Fretted Biography

The First Six Albums

by Mark Duffett

Published in 2012 by Bennion Kearny Limited.

Copyright ©Bennion Kearny Ltd 2012

ISBN: 978-1-909125-05-6

Published by Bennion Kearny Limited
6 Victory House, 64 Trafalgar Road
Birmingham, B13 8BU

www.BennionKearny.com

Cover images: ©Mark Duffett

About the Book

This book is a lightly revised edition of: *Bryan Adams: A Fretted Biography* - first released in 1994 (0952508303).

Praise for the 1994 edition:

"Overviews of other Canadian bands and artists... are included in this interesting book. Bryan Adams' successes throughout the 1980s and 1990s are well documented... Duffett makes a point of praising Adams' songwriting abilities... Overall, Duffett's biography of the 'Groover from Vancouver' Bryan Adams is well written and a fine introduction to Adams' career for most fans".
Paul Bezanker in The Record / CD/ Cassette Collectors' Exchange, May 1995

"The book impresses with facts and figures. It also explores Adams' 'regular guy' image".
Fonorama, June 1995

"Bryan Adams, A Fretted Biography is something that you don't see very often... It also contains Canadian press information on the man that was previously unavailable in the UK".
Making Music, Feb 1995

About the Author

Dr Mark Duffett is a Senior Lecturer in Media and Cultural Studies at the University of Chester. His research interests centre on celebrity images and fan phenomena. Since originally writing *Bryan Adams: A Fretted Biography*, Mark has published many articles and book chapters on popular music. He is currently working on a textbook about media fandom for Continuum.

Table of Contents

Introduction

Finding him on the radio is like discovering a mosquito buzzing in your ear, you quickly swat him away, but you know that someday you're going to have to deal with him again.
- J. Guterman and O. O'Donnel[1]

Fame is a cruel sea. Those who study the lives of public musicians often have to shift roles from being astrologers - observing the movements of stars and their impact upon peoples' lives - to becoming archaeologists who scrape the grime of history from defunct moments and recall their lost magic.

Bryan Adams' long spell in the spotlight has suggested that he has something special to offer. When Adams' label, A&M, released his greatest hits package in the early 1990s, it was hard to think that nearly a decade had passed since Bryan's most memorable effort, *Reckless*, was unleashed on a (largely) unsuspecting world. That dusty, guitar driven LP allowed him to bust through the musical ranks simply by cranking up his Strat' and delivering straight ahead rock. Even those scribes who found their hobby in cutting the Canadian rocker down to size would probably have agreed it was his best work so far.

The songs from Reckless became an ally to rack jobbers (who put cassettes in petrol stations and supermarkets), MTV programmers, and classic rock DJs alike. On the album cover Bryan peered out from a monochrome head-and-shoulders shot. In best film noire style, everything below the bridge of his nose - the rough chin, the leather jacket with upturned collar and the white tee shirt - was cast in shadow. There was a clear sky in the background and the net result was that the picture conveyed a scene and a stance. A defiant young tough is meeting us at twilight, maybe at some wilderness rendezvous point. His hair is unkempt and he's making direct eye contact with us. But despite the stare his head is turned slightly to the left (only one ear is showing) and he's not happy. It's as if he's forcing himself to meet our gaze, and maybe so squaring us up for a fight, drug deal, drag race or something similar.

Why should we pay so much attention to this little visual marketing ploy? Especially when the album itself doesn't sound quite as dark as its cover suggests, and is just a tiny fragment of popular culture disseminated across record collections in the corners of bedrooms and lounges throughout America, Europe, and elsewhere. Adams probably didn't pay much attention to his cover: it's the music that matters, right? The music does matter, but because rock'n'roll sometimes has the supernatural ability to evoke rare moments of raw emotion in the space between two speakers - from something as cold as a plastic disc - it becomes a ripe ground for fetishism. It makes other things matter: fans find themselves poring through the racks of London's big record stores, collecting every version of a release, casting long stares over their favourite album covers, scouring liner notes. They end up fighting with parents over how loud they can play records, and with their buddies over the line-ups of some long forgotten band.

Popular music has always been a festival of appropriation, a toolbox of Attitude open for anybody to use for their own ends, and that dictum applies as much to its producers as its consumers. Record labels and their artists inevitably provide us with a code - a swirling trail of minutes, a myriad of tiny indications - through which we have an opportunity to make sense of some aspects of our lives. They are as active in cobbling together images and sounds that they hope will eventually sell as we are in reclaiming those for our own intent.

Bryan Adams is living proof that the kids really do want to rock; someone who has managed to skilfully make the echo of a fraught past ring true in the blandness of the present. Yet, Adams has done it in a remarkably conservative way. Book length biographies of the superstar already exist, but they seem to be oriented towards teen fans by giving lots of pictures with an uncritical, 'factual' treatment of Bryan' s ascendance right up to the *Into The Fire* album. The aim of this work is partly to update that main story, but also to add some additional perspectives too. Such perspectives include the role of Bryan's manager, Bruce Allen, and the roots and repercussions of the whole Adams phenomenon within his home country: Canada. In fact Allen, biographer Jane O'Hara and even Canada's former environment minister have all said Bryan Adams is an ambassador for his country.[2] As we shall see, Adams' nationality has itself become used in various ways in an attempt to make a story from the man who says he's got "no image", but has paradoxically emerged as a rocker of global standing.[3]

Adams claimed a corner of popular music for himself without any sense of external purpose, and without the gimmicks and frippery that frequently went with the medium. More than a few people were left uncomfortable as Adams went against their idea of what a rock'n'roll hero should be, and where he should lead the youthful masses. The result was a hail of descriptions and criticism, without much explanation.

In the firestorm a couple of key issues were ignored. First, the question of what Adams himself was setting out to do, and how the fans had appropriated his public persona - his music, his image – has rarely been explored. Second, since rock is a forum encrusted with the clutter of years of youth culture, the implications of Bryan's activities for the genre itself have not really been examined. In a sense Adams' own conservatism, opportunism, derivativeness and popularity can be used as evidence to explore such questions. A central concern is how somebody can come along and clear a new space on the mythical landscape of rock without respect for what's already there; especially if what's already there is a sense of youth, of rebellion, of using sexuality to subvert, defy and define. This relates to the question of how much Adams *did* take up those things, how much he wanted to, and how much he *had* to do so.

This is a 'fretted' biography; fretted in the sense that Adam's popularity presented many (Adams himself included) with some dilemmas which just didn't seem to exist for previous and contemporary icons of popular culture, from Madonna to Springsteen It is perhaps also fretted in the sense (to use the slogan from *Reckless*) of playing till one's fingers bleed, in the way that a guitar solo is also a drama of anguish over questions unresolved.

The objective is to examine the public life and recording career of a star known for being so unusually usual, and from that to pull out a dialogue about what rock now might mean. Therefore the strategy is not to gossip about what Bryan Adams is "really" like, but to look at his public persona as a way to ask how much we can - and should - take from the leaders that we follow. Attention to Bryan's family background and private life have consequently been marginalised to the extent that they simply form a broad context: everything here is already knowledge in the public domain.

Bryan's career shows that people who find themselves in the spotlight don't always get an easy ride at the hands of a peripheral force like the rock press, who can hold immense, latent powers. Yet Adams' antics also show how much stars can move in the other directions, how far they can step out of the spectacle and rally the public to exert an influence on real life. In short it would be wrong to consider celebrities like Adams as prisoners stuck within the confines of the twilight zone that is popular culture. For such a supposedly regular guy, Bryan Adams has a peculiarly irregular history. That paradox itself is worth our attention.

---

[1] *Slipped Discs* (1991, p.25).

[2] O'Hara (1989, p.48); BC Report (v.3/5, 30/9/91, pp.39-40).

[3] *Rock World* (v.10/2, 1993, p.14).

1

The Early Years

He knocks on the door of his girlfriend's
house. Annie didn't think this rockaholic
gentleman offered much of a future. She had
no idea that the guy, whose name was Bryan
Adams was someday going to be... well,
Bryan Adams.

— W. Deverell[1]

For somebody who was to become one of the central figures in
1980s mainstream rock, Bryan Adams had a relatively
inauspicious beginning. His father, Conrad Adams, and his
mother Jane, emigrated to Canada from England in the 1950s.
Like his own father James, Conrad attended the Royal Military
Academy at Sandhurst, but while James fought in both world
wars, Conrad was born too late to see wartime service. He had

Chapter 1

been a soldier for Britain and then for Canada, and in keeping with his vocation went on to become a military diplomat.

Jane fell pregnant in 1959, and one day that winter, while Conrad was away in Malaya, she tenaciously walked 2 kilometres to a hospital in Kingston, Ontario, where she gave birth to a boy. Since he was born on the 5th of November, it was decided his middle name would be Guy.

Bryan Guy Adams and his younger brother Bruce had an unusual upbringing. Their father's middle level job in the Canadian Diplomatic Corps meant that the family moved at least once every three years and they had to make new friends in each new place they settled: England, Portugal, Austria, and ultimately Canada once again.

In England young Bryan was sent to a military boarding school. He liked to play soccer but was rather belligerent at times. The young upstart occasionally got suspended, and once was even expelled. Such tales might suggest that he was some kind of junior ring leader, but in fact there was another side to the youngster. Tension between his parents made things uneasy at home and probably helped to add an air of shyness and a penchant for truancy to his defiant young persona.

Adams' parents split up when he was twelve, and it seems likely that this could have affected the boy's self-esteem; he had no substantial contact with his father again for the next nine years. Once Bryan became famous, *The Sun* newspaper ran a story based on their discovery of Adams' parents' divorce papers in Ottawa. They claimed that Conrad had physically beaten his family, and because Bryan' s headmaster at the American School he attended in Tel Aviv noticed something was wrong with the boy, young Bryan had been sent to see a psychotherapist. The extent to which these insinuations were true is not as relevant here as the fact that they actually bolstered the Adams legend as a budding rebel - a moody kid firmly in the James Dean category - who found a way to channel his angst in rock music, the play world into which he could escape.

Perhaps it would be closer to the truth to consider the flip side of the situation. Bryan Adams was a supposedly shy kid, but one who really liked music, especially The Beatles. His parents had bought him drums and an acoustic guitar while his age was still in single figures. Bryan picked up an imitation Fender Stratocaster when he was just 10 and by the time of the mid-1990s he'd been playing electric guitar for over twenty years. That early start was itself a testament to his enthusiasm. If many musicians are simply people with dreams of fame and fortune, the way that Adams taught himself guitar, vocals and soon enough piano suggest those dreams were central to his young life. Similarly, stage performance is a way to be someone else and to please a group of people; Bryan formed his first band, Baker and Lawyer, while he was still at school. Since Adams has spent so much of his life on the road since then, those years were really his formative time.

In about 1974, at the age of fifteen, Bryan moved with his mother and brother to Vancouver, on the mild, wet, west coast of British Columbia. The beautiful city sprawls around English Bay and the family established themselves on its north shore in West Van', where Bryan attended the Argyle Secondary School. Although he washed dishes at the Tomahawk Restaurant for $2.50 an hour, young Mr. Adams' main effort was put into auditioning for local bands. One was being put together by Dave Taylor, a young Jimi Hendrix freak from the North Shore. At the time Taylor dismissed the pimply kid who stormed in and hammered out a few basic guitar chords as an unsuitable, an insignificant wannabe.

Chapter 1

Nevertheless the boy from West Vancouver kept trying. He quit school to play in a group called Shock, and used the $2000 fund that his parents had saved for his college education to buy a second-hand Estey grand piano upon which to tinker. At one stage, he even sold pet food to make ends meet. He got into sounds as diverse as Creedence Clearwater Revival and Deep Purple, and attended gigs by Led Zepplin, T-Rex and Elton John. Adams was bent on finding the magic ingredients that made those bands so popular, and he kept up his attempts to make connections as well. Once, to no avail, he tried to get backstage to speak with Tina Turner when she came to town.

One band that had a reasonable local following was Sweeny Todd. When they did a Vancouver gig in 1976 in the southern suburb of Surrey, the 16 year old upstart went along and claimed to Sweeny's producer that he could sing better than their front man. After an audition, he got the job. The group already had a hit on their hands with a release recorded with their former singer, Nick Gilder, called 'Roxy Roller.' It was an economic, plodding T-Rex style tune that represented a kind of Canadian answer to glam rock. Adams emulated Gilder on stage and was forced into the odd position of accepting a Juno - one of the annual awards presided over by CARAS (a body made up of the Canadian music industry) – for a single on which he had not sung. Ironically it was to be the first of many awards that he would collect.[2]

When Sweeny Todd folded (perhaps under the onslaught of punk and disco, as they were neither) Adams returned to school temporarily. At Long & McQuade music store on 4th Avenue - a street which had been a centre for hippy culture a few years earlier - he struck up a friendship with a quiet man named Jim Vallance.

Vallance was a twenty five year old local musician, born in Chilliwack, who learned to play piano from the age of seven, and completed a degree in classical cello down the road at the University of British Columbia. Since then, he had done various musical jobs. At one time he had been active in the Vancouver jingle industry, at another an apprentice sound engineer. He had also filled in as a session performer.

By 1975 Vallance had gravitated to pop and joined the group Prism, which was managed by industry entrepreneur Bruce Allen. Prism also included Bruce Fairbairn. When Allen decided that it was uneconomic to take their horn section on tour, Fairbairn found he had a talent behind the production console. Meanwhile Vallance played drums and went by the name of Rodney Higgs in case his old pals from the UBC music department spotted him in the band.

After two years Jim left Prism because he never enjoyed the pressure of public performance. The band kept going without him and stayed on friendly terms, but now the multi-talented instrumentalist was looking for a new singer with whom to form a partnership. An enthusiastic eighteen year old Bryan Adams seemed to fit the bill perfectly.

Since they are a way to convey private feelings in public places, songs can be sharp, double-edged swords for their makers. There is an element of prostitution in singing your heart out to anyone who will pay to listen, but at the same time being able to share feelings that connect with other people can be an exhilarating experience. Extrovert musicians may have an urge to communicate, but when they do many are aware of the weight of public expectation upon them. Although the new pair originally considered the name Adams and Vallance, Jim opted to be the silent partner. For Vallance, the older and more reticent member of the pair, the songs were the important thing. He constructed a small studio in his downtown home as a laboratory to create them. Vallance felt more comfortable as just a writer. He would get his rewards from that area alone without the trouble of performing and potential difficulties of being recognized offstage wherever he went. There was, consequently, little chance of an ego dispute between the two men: only one of them wanted the spotlight. The symbiotic relationship between Vallance and Adams not only had the potential to work smoothly, but to stand the test of time.

As they soon found out, the two men worked well in combination. Both had schooled themselves thoroughly in the mechanics of rock and together they particularly admired the work of Lennon and McCartney. Vallance was a dynamic keyboard player, excellent arranger and could stretch his talent to playing other instruments. He took the bass while Adams jammed on guitar. They knew they had something cooking. The dynamic duo was so very enthusiastic that, in fact, they stopped a pedestrian in the street to road-test a tape of their first song!

Then, in 1978, within a year of first teaming up, Adams found a publishing deal. After being rejected by a dozen record companies, Irving-Almo (the publishing arm of A&M Canada) offered him the token sum of $1 in return for the right to shop his songs to any interested singers and take a cut of half the resulting royalties. Desperate to break to the next level, Bryan said yes to the offer.

About this time Adams began banging on the door of a music entrepreneur named Bruce Allen, a man who had already become a key behind-the-scenes figure in the North West rock industry.

Born in 1945, Allen had begun his career in band management in the 1960s. By managing an R'n'B band called Five Man Cargo he rose to prominence in a thriving local scene. Driven towards even greater things, his ambition was to take a band beyond the Vancouver area, and he eventually got that chance with Bachman-Turner-Overdrive (BTO).

In the late 1960s, the Canadian music scene remained embryonic. Local radio stations would play bands from the US in preference to domestic outfits, because American acts had hits proven on a much larger scale. To compound the problem, major labels then avoided bands which couldn't get significant airplay on the radio, since they would not be profitable. Frequently bands that were ignored at home would overflow down into the USA and continue their struggle to be heard. Many had to wait until changes to local radio regulations encouraged their songs to be played on the air at home, but such changes did not begin until the 1970s. However, beginning in 1968, a Canadian band called The Guess Who managed to break the US charts with hit after hit, and in consequence redefined the perceived level of success that Canadian acts were thought capable of attaining.

The Guess Who's songwriters were singer Burton Cummings and guitarist Randy Bachman. In effect that pair were the forebears of the likes of Bryan Adams. After all, the group dressed informally, had unprecedented hits in the USA, and got criticized as derivative bubble-gum makers because their music particularly demonstrated its mainstream influences. Although Burton Cummings had an extraordinary voice, the man who carried the golden thread of Canadian rock forwards from this band was its barnstorming guitarist, Randy Bachman.

Cummings and Bachman did not always see eye to eye. Burton the singer was a sloppy rocker dedicated to his lifestyle of the road, while Randy was a moralist and family man. As the two climbed the ladder of fame and wealth with classics like 'American Woman' the tensions grew between them and in May

Chapter 1

1970 Bachman left the band. That same year Bruce Allen began a talent and booking agency with his Jewish business partner Sam Feldman.

With Bachman gone, Cummings and the remainder of his band enlisted a new guitarist and bounced back with an excellent Beatlesque pop platter called 'Share The Land'. Over the next few years less success in the singles charts conspired with their wild habits on tour to engineer their demise. After that, The Guess Who's irrepressible lead singer attempted an unimpressive solo career.

Meanwhile, following a spell hibernating in Winnipeg, Randy Bachman returned to the spotlight with a country rock trio which he named Brave Belt. Randy's younger brother Rob played the drums and after one largely-ignored LP, they earned a modest living by touring their native country. Brave Belt ended up in Vancouver, under the management of Bruce Allen, where they received rejections from all the majors before being favourably reconsidered by the Mercury label. Another member of the Bachman family, Tim, was enlisted on rhythm guitar and after that the group changed their name to Bachman-Turner-Overdrive in honour of their bass playing vocalist Fred Turner. With a new label and more populist approach, BTO was re-invigorated. They were looking for stardom.

BTO's first album was a minor hit, selling about 235,000 units across North America. Since their singles made AM radio playlists, they generated enough momentum for Mercury to ship 100,000 copies of their next LP to eager retailers before its release date.

By 1974 BTO were really hitting the big time: they had several chart singles, the best two of which were 'You Ain't Seen Nothing Yet' and 'Taking Care of Business.' And Mr. Bachman was certainly taking care of it. As a writer he may have been one of rock's best minimalists, but as a musician he was a commercial opportunist of the highest calibre. Randy was even churning out plodding rock tunes that he didn't particularly care for. Whatever sounded commercial was grist to the mill; 'Taking Care of Business' itself was based on a radio jingle that one day got stuck in his head! Nevertheless the kids lapped it up. Despite Bachman's opportunism, fans (especially in Canada) took to his music almost like a cause in itself.

From the evidence available, it seems that Bruce Allen had always been intensely driven and ambitious - a character with a sharp eye on the entertainment business - and he was always ready with an opinion. In 1975, at the peak of BTO-mania, Allen accompanied the group on a 10 city, 13 date Canadian tour which netted them $1.5 million; a staggering figure for the time. The crucial thing about the BTO tour was that Allen learned about the real practice of pleasing crowds by observing his band; it was a kind of apprenticeship for him.

The last half of the decade was a time of difficulty and great change for Allen. Although he took up Prism, after Bachman left BTO in 1977 the band fell apart, so Allen's main act was no more. Also that year, Sam Feldman, who became strained from working with such an overpowering partner, left with his booking agency (which took $1 million annually in those days). He and Allen remained legally bound together so they could continue to share in each other's profits.

Despite these setbacks, Allen's track record left him as the most important music industry figure in Vancouver. He had three vital ingredients to help any budding talent that he chose to take on: working capital, contacts within the industry, and an aggressive approach to shopping his clients to the major labels.

Chapter 1

Bryan Adams had been pestering Bruce Allen for a whole year before anything really happened. Absorbed in his existing business concerns, Allen just didn't want to know. Eventually, in December 1979, the manager capitulated. He had already overseen Jim Vallance in Prism and he knew Vallance had talent. Furthermore, his new charge had predicted "I'll be the biggest act you ever have" and Allen knew that he meant it.[3] Bruce sent Bryan a contract laying down the standard 15% manager's fee, but Adams never signed it; trust was enough.

Adams' publishing deal with A&M gave him immense freedom. It meant that a kid, still in his teens, was given the opportunity to express himself to a wider audience. That set the stage for Bryan Adams to spend his twenties literally growing up on record.

In 1979, a year after his publishing contract began, Adams' label lifted the song 'Let Me Take You Dancing' from a 4 track demo, remixed it, and sped it up at the label's New York studios ready for release. The song became a minor disco hit, setting alight dance floors in Montreal, New York and Paris; eventually it sold around 240,000 copies, but it was a rather embarrassing beginning.

Adams and Vallance steeped themselves in conventional pop and rock influences so they were not primarily orientated towards the disco market. Their squeaky platter became the dubious hook around which early tales of the emergence of Bryan Adams could be written. Yet, apart from the royalty cheques from A&M, even 'Let Me Take You Dancing' had an advantage: it meant that at only 19 years old, Bryan Adams had emerged as a vocalist in his own right. However, it was still several years before his success in that direction was to eclipse his role as a writer for other more famous artists.

While Adams had underground disco success, his manager was more concerned with shaping up another act new to his books: Loverboy.

Loverboy's story started across the Rockies in Calgary where Lou Blair, who ran the Refinery Nightclub, took charge of a veteran guitarist named Paul Dean. Aged thirty three, Dean had been knocking about in Canadian bands for several years. In the 1960s he'd been part of the Vancouver-based outfit Kenny Dean and The Chantells, who were another of the bands bringing alive the North West's R'n'B scene. More recently he had enjoyed success as the leader of Winnipeg's finest hard rock group, Streetheart: a band which, amongst other things, cracked the US market with a cover of the Stones' tune 'Under My Thumb'. Blair spent time clearing Dean of outstanding legal contracts (a process known as 'cleaning up' in the business), after which he presented the musician to Allen in a bid to engineer a co-management arrangement.

The two men struck up a deal which would work because, in general, Blair kept out of the way. Allen was left to construct a band that could respond well to salient market forces. He attempted to engineer their image in a way that would maximize profits in light of where he thought the industry was going and based on what he had learned from BTO. The strategy was to appeal to young girls, take full advantage of the emergent medium of video, and provide hard rock anthems for the masses.

Dean was an old hand - Loverboy was his 14th band - so together with singer Mike Reno he chose the rest of the group's members as much for their good looks as for their musical abilities. Allen told them how to dress (choosing bright reds and yellows), the order in which to play their songs at gigs, and he even tutored them on topic effective between-song patter. The band's members initially called their alliance The Project, in deference to its money-making potential. Their whole approach to rock was a highly calculated pretence.

After rejections from nearly two dozen record companies CBS decided to give Loverboy a try, so they recorded an album that the label released in Canada during 1980. As the experiment was successful, the album was unleashed on America the following year. Allen kept Loverboy particularly well regimented and was in the habit of paying his bands a salary while investing the rest of the money they made. In 1981 his band did 250 dates without any set changes; they stuck closely to the formula that they had hit upon. The next year Allen made a $1 million deal with Nissan Automobiles to sponsor their tour, which consisted of another 240 dates. Soon a string of hit singles, hit albums and a loyal fan base had secured fame and fortune for the boys. To organize his finances that year Dean alone employed 4 lawyers, 2 accountants and a bookkeeper! Allen had got his formula spot on target, Loverboy captured a loyal clutch of fans and the group became a huge success. Even their t-shirts were so lucrative that the group formed their own manufacturing company rather than take the usual option of a royalty cut from profits made by other operators.

Loverboy had found the magic formula that let them coast on into the mid-1980s. Their albums were usually produced by Bruce Fairbairn in Vancouver's Little Mountain Sound Studios, and their production sound was so good that other rockers sat up, took notice, and came from all over the USA. Those who could afford it arranged to record their own material at the studio, and gave Bob Rock (who began behind the console as a sound engineer) and Bruce Fairbairn a nice, steady income. The pair helped several top bands to capture a characteristic metal sound in the studio. Arguably the most important group they assisted was Bon Jovi, who recorded their breakthrough album 'Slippery When Wet' in Vancouver during 1983.

The success of Little Mountain Sound meant that Bruce Allen came up trumps. As well as managing Loverboy, he represented Fairbairn and Rock. However, that emerging solo singer he had taken on, the one named Bryan Adams, was (relatively speaking) still in the shadows.

---

[1] *Saturday Night* (v.107/9, 11/92 p.55-56).

[2] CARAS is the Canadian Academy of Recording Arts and Sciences. To this day they promote the national Juno awards for musicians and the Canadian Music Hall of Fame.

[3] *Maclean's* magazine (v.100/27, 6/7/87 p.33).

2

The First Three Albums

When 1983 was over, Loverboy had grossed $46 million on tour, with a further $6 million taken in merchandise sales. Allen's cut from all of that added considerably to his own mountain of wealth. Against the spiralling background of Vancouver's rock industry, another of the manager's charges, a young Bryan Adams, began to plot his own exponential growth trajectory. Like many similar journeys it was, at first, disappointingly slow.

To capitalize on the success of his disco single, A&M subsidized Adams to the tune of $100,000 so he could make an album. With the eponymous title of 'Bryan Adams' it was recorded in Toronto, with Vallance behind the production console and a plethora of session musicians backing up the young singer. The whole thing was mixed in LA, packaged with a garish purple and blue cover shot and yet it went on to become a hit in Canada (selling 50,000 units) but nowhere else.

From the beginning the entire venture had been risky and it certainly didn't leave Adams rich. Even after the first album was released he had to do jingles for department stores like The Bay to make ends meet. On a more positive note, Bryan now had something concrete on the LP racks of record stores everywhere to show he had arrived as a professional artist. Since Loverboy were proving more lucrative as a strike force of rock'n'roll mercenaries than even Allen and Blair had hoped for, Allen could keep the pressure off Adams if the career of his young prodigy was not going too well.

Besides, Vallance and Adams were becoming fine songwriters who made up in quality what their output lacked in quantity. Between 1979 and 1981 they penned some 40 songs together, most of which went to outside artists. Irving-Almo's aggressive sales policy and willingness to accept a lower royalty rate than was standard helped disseminate this Adams / Vallance material across an international marketplace. If the songs had been rubbish, even a discount would not have sold them. A line of famous customers for material made by the pair proved that they could deliver good tunes and because Ian Lloyd had a minor hit with 'Lonely Nights,' (a composition penned by the duo) they began to get more media attention.

Since the first album had basically flopped, a frustrated Adams toyed with the idea of calling his second effort 'Bryan Adams Hasn't Heard of You Either' but he settled on 'You Want It You Got It.' He visited studios in Montreal and Vancouver during the spring of 1981 to record the LP with the New York-based producer Bob Clearmountain, a rock veteran who had previously worked with such luminaries as The Rolling Stones and Roxy Music. A&M released the resulting collection of songs in an album with Adams, now twenty two, wearing a casual jacket and t-shirt and smiling meekly from its cover. From there it was a matter of finding every opportunity to promote the new platter.

At that stage Adams was rather stuck, because he had no band but needed one to showcase his new album at Toronto's live music club El Morcambo. He quickly set about auditioning musicians in the Vancouver area. The guitarists that he picked were Dave Taylor – the same man who had rejected Bryan's application to join his band a few years earlier - on bass, and Keith Scott on lead. Scott had been a minor local celebrity and an old rival of Adams in his early days on the Vancouver music scene. In the meantime he had recorded with a Jazz fusion outfit signed to a British indie label, but they had folded when disco became popular. Bryan Adams now had a road band pulled together from the cream of the local crop. Eventually they went by the name of The Dudes of Leisure.

1982 was spent writing more songs and touring North America for much of the time. It was, above all, a year in which Bryan Adams learned to work an audience with his simple, enthusiastic stage act.

Allen carefully arranged it so that his boy opened for some major artists: Bryan did 68 shows opening for Foreigner, 30 for The Kinks, and a considerable number for Loverboy, including one in front of 22,000 fans in Toronto. Adams proved immensely popular and was too dynamic an opener for many bands to tolerate. Bryan frequently stole the show, winning the support of fans who had come to see the headliner acts. He suggested to one interviewer at the time: "I go all the way. In the last four months I've learned to go absolutely nuts and be able to take an audience from not knowing who I am to going out and buying my albums."[1] The proof of the pudding was in the fact that the talented young rocker earned respectable sales figures for his second major vinyl outing, which attained platinum status in his native country by shifting 150,000 copies.

Chapter 2

Meanwhile the Adams / Vallance song writing factory was busy exporting more material. Many of the efforts that they sent away were a bit limp, such as 'Don't Let Him Know' which was released by Prism. Significantly, any songs penned by the duo qualified as Canadian in content under national radio regulations. This meant that even if those compositions were sung by foreign artists, they were more likely to get played on Canadian radio stations than material created outside of Canada. Even if the songs written by Adams and Vallance did not always become hits in the hands of non-domestic artists, the Canadian radio rule probably increased the size of royalty cheques the Vancouver-based pair received.

Furthermore, to advance the music which Bryan released himself, Adams became a pleasant PR man, courteously working radio stations on his tour path, even suggesting hooks and headlines for journalists who wished to cover his emergent phenomenon. He became *Today* magazine's face of '82 and was widely-tipped for bigger things.

The prediction began to come true in 1983, when Adams, Allen, and A&M joined forces in a concerted effort to break the Canadian singer-songwriter outside his home country. In a move which was unusual for an artist, Adams made sure that he became friends on a personal level with the inhabitants of the upper echelons of A&M's head office down in the USA. His rapport worked in parallel with Allen's efforts to persuade the label down the phone line. Allen and Adams must have been like a good cop / bad cop team in their attempts to lobby A&M. The artist would turn up in LA to press flesh and explain he was working hard on everybody's behalf then, later, his manager would phone from Vancouver to urge them into devoting more attention and resources towards his boy. The combination was probably the way it had to be, especially since the added costs of video promotion meant each act took more budget, and major labels were quite often reticent to prioritize stars based outside their administrative territories. Allen had built his empire from Vancouver, a satellite city in a satellite country as far as the majors were concerned. With Adams, he was probably the only person living locally with enough connections to make a star. Now, thanks to both men's efforts, A&M was right behind its twenty three year old budding recording star.

Everyone from Bonny Raitt to Uriah Heap had already bought songs Adams had crafted with Jim Vallance. The two men had supplied material to over twenty other artists in different music genres. Now the problem was to decide which songs to sell. Which songs were better suited to the styles of other acts? Which songs to keep for Adams' next album? Perhaps the danger was that after selling off so much material, Bryan might have been left without a style of his own. While he had recorded diverse pop and ballad-type material for previous album releases, for his new album, Adams took on a sharper Album Oriented Rock sound.

In early 1983 his third album, *Cuts Like A Knife,* was released after being recorded at Little Mountain Sound in Vancouver. Adams co-produced the suite of songs with Bob Clearmountain, who took on the sound engineering and mixing duties. Bob moved the mixing job to Le Studio in Morrin Heights and completed it back on his turf at the Power Station in New York.

The *Cuts Like A Knife* line-up was typical: Mickey Curry pounding out the beat (with occasional percussion from Vallance); Scott and Taylor on the rhythm section; Tommy Mandel on keyboards and Adams either administering his intense front vocals or sharing guitar solos with Keith Scott. Lou Gramm from Foreigner had seen the band displaying their talent on tour when they opened for his group and ended up guesting on backing vocals for the new album. In retrospect it was an indication of Adams' emergent musical direction.

Since it was the album which broke Bryan Adams on a wider market and gave him a sense of future direction, *Cuts Like A Knife* is the first of his records worthy of critical attention here. It was the first album which gave you a distinct feeling that Bryan Adams had an ability to press your emotional buttons, but many of the songs - mostly Adams / Vallance compositions - were not together enough; they slid between blandness and vaudeville. Nonetheless the talent could be heard, from the gauche awkwardness of the first verse of 'The Only One' to that resigned monologue which constituted the title track. 'Let Him Know' found the Adams' band in a distinctly retro, almost Motown mood.

One ballad called 'Straight From The Heart' was also recorded with more of a gospel tinge by the raunchy Welsh singer Bonnie Tyler. The song held its own when it appeared on her album later that year next to material written by Meatloaf's old Svengali, Jim Steinman. However the skill displayed was not only in the song writing. In fact Adams had an ability to throw himself into the roles opened up by his songs like some kind of bewitched method actor. He believed in what he was singing and at times made otherwise marginal tunes grow in their appeal and really connect. All in all, *Cuts Like A Knife* was a reasonably good effort: often heartfelt, occasionally hammy, but well above the standard of most acts. Perhaps its biggest disadvantage was that the album, if taken as a whole, distinctly lacked direction. Nevertheless, the LP added a new tinge of rock to Adams' vinyl persona.

Perhaps the two tracks most indicative of what was to follow were the urgent 'Don't Leave Me Lonely' and the Stonesy number 'Take Me Back'. Those songs clearly showed Adams could rock when he wanted and his marketing team wasted no time in giving visual reference to the fact. On the album's cover was a rough around the edges, full length, indoor shot of young Bryan. He was highly posed; doing some kind of jerky dance with a guitar in hand. It was the first time he sported a leather jacket, but certainly not the last. The garment, which already connoted 1950s-style rock rebellion, became identified with Adams in future photos as a visual trademark. On an inside shot he stood squarely with it zipped right up. Almost grinning down towards the camera, Bryan looked like some kind of biker, shop mannequin, or a member of the Police (with whom he had toured Australia and New Zealand that year). The intention was clear: Bryan Adams the rocker had arrived.

And he toured. Almost constantly. Adams did 100 US dates in five months, opening for Aerosmith and Journey, followed by a six week tour of Europe. Then he went on to the Southern hemisphere!

A&M had sunk around $1.5 million into the whole Bryan Adams circus, and thankfully it was now all coming together. While it would be nice to believe that Adams' hard work on the road was what paid off - he spent 283 days touring, including a three month spell on Toronto's Yonge Street at one stage - other factors were at play.

Even if Adams now appeared like a rocker, he was an unusual one, because he could handle ballads with outstanding intensity. Since A&M knew that the slow numbers were the strongest contenders on *Cuts Like A Knife*, they released those ones as singles. The album's title track had a controversial video directed by Steve Barron which was picked out by MTV and its exposure moved Adams up to number 15 in the Billboard singles chart. With the extra media attention that Bonnie Tyler's cover of 'Straight From The Heart' received, the song made it to number

10 when sung by its writer. At last Adams was beginning to crack the US market: his album had reached number 8 on the Billboard chart and sold a million copies in America by the end of the year. It went on to gradually sell another million units across that territory, and a total of 330,000 copies also went in Canada. Sales were marginal in Britain, however, since Adams' hits had not happened on the other side of the Atlantic. The net result was that, after six years of trying, Bryan Adams was storming the US charts.

1983 ended on a high. Allen had seen both of his major groups solidly work their way forward to become immense successes; Adams won a Juno for best male vocalist and was even compared to the year's best selling US rocker, John Cougar Mellencamp. He had also been commissioned to write the theme song for a new movie starring Christopher Atkins called 'A Night in Heaven'. It was to be the start of a new and even better chapter.

---

[1] *Winnipeg Free Press* (12/5/82, p.28).

3

Reckless

What makes heroic? - To go to meet
simultaneously one's greatest sorrow and
greatest hope.

- Friedrich Nietzsche[1]

In 1984 Bryan Adams was under the gun to follow up the
success of his previous album with an offering that would be at
least as popular. His label A&M realized that the media interest
generated in America by the singles from *Cuts Like A Knife* would
not build unless more great material was forthcoming. As it
stood, despite being an excellent stage performer, Adams' nearly
constant touring in the years before that album were relatively
fruitless in terms of selling records. It was his exposure on the
TV, radio, and across the pages which really mattered.

Chapter 3

With a couple of big singles in the USA acting as its advertisements, *Cuts Like A Knife* soon shifted well over a million copies which was a respectable figure for an emergent artist. At the same time, Britain still hadn't really heard of Bryan Adams, despite his continental success on the other side of the world. It was time to write new songs and build on what was previously learned to make a new album.

Nestling amongst the North West's vast forests, below snowy mountains and sprawling before the sea, Vancouver is a bustling, cosmopolitan city. At its urban core the sky scrapers and well regulated streets offer a laid back, affluent, cosmopolitan atmosphere that exists near to alternative districts characterized by beggars, strip clubs and drunks. On his song writing forays, Adams would drive down from his rented bungalow on the north shore, over the Lions Gate Bridge towards the heart of the city.

He would stop at the house where Vallance lived with his wife Rachel Paiement, a former member of the theatrical French Canadian rock troop CANO. The two men would jam into their 16 track home studio, the usual configuration being Adams on lead and Vallance on bass, working for up to 12 hours each session.

Bryan was slightly better at lyrics and his lines often inspired melodies for songs. Although the pair only averaged 10 songs together per year between 1978 and 1985, 90% of their compositions were recorded by one artist or another: they had a phenomenal success rate. In typical fashion, aside from their own album, 1984 saw Adams and Vallance pen two tracks for the film 'Teachers' which starred Nick Nolte: 'Teacher, Teacher,' released by .38 Special, and 'Edge Of A Dream,' sung by Joe Cocker.

Called *Reckless* to convey its jagged rock temperament, the new album was finally released in October. Again the recording venue had been Little Mountain Sound with Adams and Clearmountain firmly behind the production console and a line-up that was more or less the same as before. Lou Gramm of Foreigner turned up to help on backing vocals, a couple of extra drummers (Pat Stewart and Steve Smith) were drafted in on the tracks where Mickey Curry didn't play, and Tina Turner finally arrived (probably thanks to Allen pulling a few strings) to duet with Bryan on 'It's Only Love'.

Although the line-up was similar to before, the new album represented a distinct shift of tone and direction. Save for a lump-in-the-throat fourth track, 'Heaven', written for the film of that name, the ballads of *Cuts Like A Knife* were now gone.

'Heaven' was such a strong song, rendered with such a heartfelt intensity of feeling, that it was to remain essential listening long after the film had been forgotten. The brilliant ballad proved an exception as it complemented a stomping set of gritty numbers. While the keyboards were still audible on some tracks, they were kept down in the mix in favour of some blazing – but well placed – guitar histrionics. It seemed that Adams and Vallance had come up with a collection of economical, up tempo rock anthems: the sort of classics that guaranteed their hoarse singer a place in the rock'n'roll hall of fame.

In a decade when live albums were almost invariably doctored in the studio, it was timely to make a studio album that *sounded* live. Some clever, sparse arrangements, guitar-oriented mixing and clear vocals gave the LP its live feel. It was as if the songs were robust enough to stand up for themselves despite being thrown together so roughly. Keith Scott simply plugged his Telecasters and Stratocasters into Marshall Amps and hammered out some memorable solos and fills with a very natural, fluent kind of dynamism. Aided by Bryan's low, edgy vocals the combination was knock out.

Adams had an ability to make the simplest of chords ring clear as bells: the opening of 'It's Only Love' became a real mantra for an otherwise bleak late '80s. The Vancouver singer-songwriter had discovered how to deliver tight, well-structured rock - charged with bad boy nostalgia but maintaining a polished level of production nevertheless. And it worked. *Reckless* was an album with so few duff tracks on, it was unbelievable. Because of that it contributed to a wider change. In years past, albums were seen by most bands either as an opportunity to explore concepts in more depth than was possible in a short time, or as a way to capitalize on a couple of singles by adding some filler. The idea of the rock LP formed as a collection of singles had now arrived, and Adams' new album was a paradigm example. Since *Reckless* proved even more consistently good than ZZ Top's *Eliminator*, the fans really liked it. In fact, as an artefact that demonstrated how excellence could be regularly achieved, it was on a par with Bon Jovi's *Slippery When Wet*, the metal masterpiece which was recorded in the same studio the year before.

Between its late October release and the year-end count up, *Reckless* went triple platinum in Canada. Bryan swept the Juno awards in early December, collecting them for top producer, best male vocalist, top album and (jointly with Vallance) for top composer. As 1984 drew to a close, a triumphant Adams was eager to hit the road again. He even cut short his holiday break with Vallance in Barbados to begin tour preparations in a Seattle rehearsal hall.

To coincide with this flurry of self-promotion, January saw the release of a video containing singles from *Reckless* made by the director of Michael Jackson's 'Billie Jean' and filmed mostly around Vancouver.

'Kids Wanna Rock' had been shot downtown at The Orpheum back in November and 'Summer of '69' provided a cheeky romp through the industrial wastelands beyond Gastown. Part of the footage for 'Run To You' was shot across the Atlantic in London, and during the filming Bryan met Vicki Russell, the daughter of the famous movie director Ken Russell, who worked as a film costumier. It was to be the start of a close relationship lasting several years. By the end of 1985, Adams had completed a year-long headlining tour which included 26 countries. Amazingly, when all his gigs are totalled up, Bryan Adams spent an average of around 250 days per year on the road for the first half of the 1980s.

Bruce Allen always had an eye to the business side of things, so he wanted Bryan to hit the baby boomers as the largest target audience available. As such, the Bryan Adams / Tina Turner collaboration episode was a calculated career move. With Vallance, Adams wrote a track for Turner's album called 'Back Where You Started' and he produced it as well, but the whole approach was largely the wrong means to Allen's end. If previously Adams had been vaguely taking pot shots at the general public of music buyers, *Reckless* had more squarely hit the MTV generation rock audience, a younger and more specific market segment. Adams' album endeared him to kids who really wanted to rock and he was one of them; a rookie by all counts.

Tina Turner had an older following. The press played up the possibility of sexual antics between the two singers, but Turner was at least twenty years Adams' senior. She was also so jaded by her previous experiences that she could only laugh him off as a cheeky kid: 'Dennis the Menace'. Similarly, it would have been difficult for Turner's older fans to accept a rock tutorial from a young upstart like Bryan. They listened with the curiosity that comes from hearing someone who sounds older than his years and recognized their favourite bands echoing through the songs he delivered.

A survey closely scrutinized by Allen (and reported in Billboard magazine) found that Adams had a mixed audience, with roughly equal numbers of girls and guys, but most of them were much younger than the baby boomer cohort. So far, then, Allen's plot to hit the jackpot had been foiled.

On the positive side, *Reckless* bought Bryan Adams a specific sort of wide recognition, and, of course, money. By that time Bryan's career had reached a stage where he was comfortable despite big overheads. To launch the album A&M charged $325,000 to a recoupable account to be paid in record sales, while the tour operation (comprising 40 staff and loads of equipment) cost $100,000 per week to keep on the road. Despite this, Adams was able to move out of his bungalow and into a 1930s mansion house nearby in the Lynn Valley, parking his BMW in front of it.

In February Bryan played on the US TV program *Saturday Night Live*. The show was not only a sure sign proving he'd arrived in the collective consciousness of the American public, it was also a chance for one ordinary guy turned superhero to meet another - Adams shook hands with Christopher Reeve, the actor who played Superman.

While Bruce Allen spent much of his time fussing over Adams on tour, he characteristically had other pots on the boil. In the previous year he'd released around $600,000 in interest-free loans to various acts who had persuaded him of their potential. Tom Cochrane, the old singer with Canadian troopers Red Rider, had been dropped from Allen's roster as a dead loss once he was $1 million in debt to his record company. Yet Bruce still had acts such as the Payola$ (a New Wave pop duo consisting of Bob Rock and Paul Hyde) and Raymond May on his books. Even

Randy Berswick – Adams' road manager and a key member of Allen's Water Street office team –took a turn by managing Barney Bentall, a struggling rocker who made it on to the A&M bargain basement series under the name of Brandon Wolf.

Although the smaller bands on his books were not paying off, Bruce Allen's central commitments were soaring into profit. Feldman's booking agency was growing steadily while Allen had increased his joint activities with Lou Blair by dabbling in the night club business. As well as their bands, the two entrepreneurs co-owned Vancouver's Club Soda and Richards On Richards nightspots. Loverboy were not doing too badly either, even though their sales were now eclipsed by young Bryan. In 1985 CBS released an album they made called *Loving Every Minute Of It* with a killer title track crafted by the songwriter-producer who had coached Def Leppard in the art of fine writing, Mutt Lange. It was not the last time one of Allen's acts would cross Lange's path.

Soon after performing on *Saturday Night Live* Adams returned to Vancouver. Allen had organized a session aimed at making a Canadian musical contribution to the cause of famine relief. An array of song writing talent was assembled to compose a tune for release as the fund-raising publicity single. Adams and Vallance supplied the lyrics and the top songwriter-arranger Dave Foster (originally an inhabitant of Victoria, who moved to LA to work for stars like Whitney Houston) created the melody. Bob Rock and Paul Hyde suggested the title of 'Tears Are Not Enough' and Jim Vallance's wife even lent a hand in the writing process. With Foster enlisted to produce the session, some 52 Canadian artists turned up to sing the composition on the day.

By November 'Tears Are Not Enough' had sold so many copies at home it raised $2.5 million for African famine relief. Although it was a response to the efforts of other national music industries, it also became an empowering step for Adams and Vallance. The song not only showed that they could please an audience but by placing their work in an appropriate context it suggested that they might begin to change the world. More parochially, 1985 had developed into an amazing year in the life of Bryan, as A&M unleashed a string of chart-busting singles. Although it's true to say that no songs from *Reckless* (or his next album) did as well in the UK as in the North American charts, 'Run To You' became Adams' first hit in Britain.

'Run To You' was a moody track, originally designed as a vehicle for the Blue Oyster Cult, but recorded by Bryan himself in the end. When 'Heaven' was released A&M could deliver the song to any format of radio station and expect to get airplay: it was such a strong ballad. In June the single became the first track by a Canadian artist to reach the top of the American Billboard chart since Anne Murray' s 1978 song 'You Needed Me,' sending out a wave of national pride north of the border.

When Adams returned home for two Vancouver dates in early September, he was given a hero's welcome: 13,000 tickets for one of the shows had sold out within 90 minutes. Later that month the rocker was greeted with similar euphoria at the Canadian National Exhibition centre in Toronto, where Adams did his stuff in front of 45,000 Canadian fans. Interestingly, Englishman John Parr who was number 1 in Canada at the time with the theme from 'St. Elmo's Fire' was the opening act. The power of Bryan Adams to excite national feelings - even though his music never sounded distinctly Canadian - was so strong that even Parr cashed-in by coming on stage with a guitar painted with the maple leaf flag. It seemed that Bryan Adams was celebrated with fervour as a homecoming road warrior; somebody who had taken on the Americans at their own game and had done better than them.

Reckless had worked its magic by the end of the year, with A&M watching money piling up in the bank every step of the way. The album reached Billboard's number one slot in August, making Adams the first Canadian act to manage the feat since BTO, who conquered America a decade earlier. The Groover from Vancouver had become the first foreign writer to have six hit singles off a bestselling album, joining an elite coterie of US artists like Michael Jackson and Lionel Ritchie. By September 1985 *Reckless* had sold 700,000 copies in Canada and 3 million in the US, but it closed the year with another 50,000 on the Canadian total and around 6 million in worldwide sales. That success stood the test of time: by 1987 Adams' album had spent 18 months on the LP charts with sales of around 10 million globally. The record had a timeless quality - a mark of good writing based upon close attention to classic influences - which meant it held its own in a sea of flimsy rock fashions. Adams' album proved to have longevity of appeal rivalling even Meatloaf's magnum opus *Bat Out Of Hell*.

In a rather clever marketing move, Adams recorded a catchy oddball single called 'Diana' questioning why, over in Britain, Lady Diana had ended up with Prince Charles. The song was first released in the UK and helped to endear the cocky rocker to British fans. Following that it was released in Canada, since Canadians are avid royal watchers as part of the Commonwealth. Even though it was a joke and never made it on to Bryan's album, along with 'Tears Are Not Enough' , the 'Diana' single was a portent: it showed Adams was not afraid of trying to intervene directly in controversies outside the world of rock'n'roll.

Meanwhile, Jim Vallance had not been sitting idle while his counterpart was away on tour. He had written songs for The Guess Who's old frontman Burton Cummings, he had also helped .38 Special again, and almost entirely masterminded the award-winning first album from Glass Tiger, a band who roared out of the Toronto area. Also Heart (the Wilson Sister's band which first hit the charts years earlier from a base in Vancouver) had taken up a number called 'What About Love' which Vallance wrote and recorded with the band Toronto back in 1981, and which they scored a big hit with.

When Adams got a break from the road, he and Vallance joined forces once more to write a couple of tracks for The Who's perennial lead singer, Roger Daltrey. Daltrey received a tune from the awestruck duo called 'Let Me Down Easy.' He was another big name they could add to their list of customers.

With success abroad came further recognition at home, from within the Canadian music industry. In October Adams and Vallance received the Harold Moon award from Canada's main performing rights society for their international achievements as Canadian songwriters. While CARAS - the body governing Canada's national music awards - had already given Bryan an armful of Juno awards for his barnstorming album in the previous year, they felt moved enough to vote for some more to go his way in 1985. A pattern which seemed almost unbreakable continued; while Adams was nominated for single of the year with 'Diana' he was pipped at the post, but got recognized as top male vocalist, composer (jointly with Vallance) and awarded for the album of the year. Also, south of the border, the Groover from Vancouver got two Grammy nominations. It was a characteristic end to a triumphant year. North America's premiere rookie rocker had burst into the public eye.

---

[1] *The Gay Science* (1882, p.275).

4

The Boy Next Door

People don't know Bryan, they just see the 'boy next door' image, the kid with the infectious grin.

- Jim Vallance[1]

So far the rise of Bryan Adams has been portrayed in terms of a select supporting cast of characters - Bruce Allen, Jim Vallance, A&M etc. - who catapulted the singer to fame in the early 1980s. That approach to writing a biography can be myopic and potentially misleading since it ignores the wider environment. The activities of rockers do not exist in a vacuum, but in a context which includes their fans, the press, their musical predecessors and idols, and any other things which shape their ascendance and acceptability.

Chapter 4

By the 1980s rock stars were not so much manufactured by their record companies as picked up for distribution by them, as long as they had music and an image which connected with the audience. The process raises a question: what forces in society - what wider precedents and tensions - make a particular image work? In short, why was a figure like Bryan Adams of use in anybody's life? To answer this question, and before considering how Bryan's image is interpreted, it is important to look at how Bruce Allen saw his act and indeed how the singer saw himself.

From his Water Street office facility, by 1985, Allen had become a Canadian celebrity in his own right. He had a reputation as the man who swung at a punch bag to relieve his executive stress, and who had an office full of pot plants that looked the other way. It was even claimed, once, that he mostly employed women because they didn't have large egos which would interfere with his demands. Certainly his business was run one way: orders came from the top down.

In turn, Adams' mentor had a highly specific philosophy that structured the adrenaline charged phone calls and 14 hour days he put into managing his acts. In fact he argued that Canada had a shortage of good managers and those who were around took too few risks. They rarely set up tours of the USA for their lesser known bands, for example. On the subject of what made a good manager Allen argued that in the music business the music was the least important ingredient, so those in his position should attend to business matters only. Personal administration was off the list of managers' duties, along with other forms of interference. Bruce Allen's stance was that because he knew nothing about actually making music, he would keep his ears out of the recording studio. Accordingly, his charges could hardly expect to tell him how to run his end of the bargain. And a bargain it was: in effect Allen only had a handshake to rely on until Bryan came up with an album each time, and the process sometimes took longer than others.

Allen saw Adams as his retirement policy. The most telling statement about an almost paternal relationship between the two men comes when Bruce complained to the press, "hit him and it hurts me."[2] In fact, it was almost as though Allen was promoting a prize boxer. Throughout the 1980s Bruce was so concerned about his boy that he constantly turned up on the road to make sure everything was going smoothly. His master plan was to tap into the baby boomer audience and let his key act contest a larger prize. Not least since, on vinyl, Adams spent the 1980s gradually growing up, and for a long time *it was not to be*. Allen always kept up his boasts that his boy was going to deliver next time, despite press indifference or speculation.

The reason Allen had so much faith in his act can be pinned down to something rather old fashioned: talent. After all, Bruce had taken charge of Adams since before the young Canuck was famous; it was not a case of buying out an already proven commodity. Allen realized Bryan had a special ability to write and sing his own songs, in the classic tradition from Cole Porter to Elton John, albeit in a new setting. In a way he was right, but that view ignored the fact that fans also supported other acts - from Bob Dylan to The Sex Pistols - not because of their musical talent, but because they each had something particular to convey. As acts, each of them had a charged image that deeply connected with their respective audiences. Paradoxically, as we shall see, Bryan himself fell into the abyss between the two modes of appeal.

The Adams / Vallance song writing partnership kept everything simple. Adams described what he wrote as third generation R'n'B. The partners made up in formal excellence what they lacked in originality and, until the mid-1980s, avoided social issues. Adams once described song writing as "what I like best... the most gratifying thing" since having a hit song meant he had convincingly appealed to people.[3] But Bryan took to performing his work because "people don't care about writers; all they care about is a hit song."[4] It was performers, rather than writers, who were recognized as worthy of attention within the rock spectacle; singing in public was where Adams' own aspirations lay. The interesting thing, in a strange kind of way, was that he forced himself into exile and then wrote autobiographical songs from right out there.

Carefully, Bryan would road test his songs to gauge audience reactions. He used his tours as a way to learn what worked as much as a forum to provide it. The set was a distinctly no-frills event: no pyrotechnics, acrobatics, no inflatables or fancy lights. Nobody went to see art-rock theatre or to overdose on metal excess at an Adams gig. The pleasure was more righteously simple: the focus was on the band and the band was tight. Rather than springing out like the mechanism of a broken watch, Keith Scott's guitar solos were tucked back into the songs, indicating his ego was subsumed in the task in hand. Similarly, each gig was no wayward jam session; there was none of the measured anarchy of, say, a soul collective. The rest of the band got behind Adams like he was their brawny gang leader.

The lack of frippery was like an actor going on stage without any props; it showed what could be achieved with just the voice alone. Bryan Adams' songs were effective emotional vehicles, machines concerned with relationships, and each performance was a microcosm - a tiny melodrama - focusing on a rough voice which suggested that its owner was someone who had done a lot of living. Adams' extraordinary vocals sounded a bit like sandpaper rubbed over wood. His raspy crooning and hoarse shouts were so low that they needed delay in the speakers not to clash with Dave Taylor's bass. Every date was set up with the one calculated intention of making Adams' songs connect with their audience. For Bryan himself, this was the main - and perhaps only - way that he received emotional gratification.

Bruce Allen's hero was the manager of Elvis Presley, Colonel Tom Parker. Parker had seen that Elvis had lower record sales every time he opened his mouth for an interview. In effect it proved that the real singer could not live up to the myth conveyed by his persona on stage or on record. The Colonel realized that if Elvis said nothing then the fans would have no reason to be disappointed, so the King remained virtually silent for the last 15 years of his career. Allen advised his acts to do the same. However, the ploy only worked for Elvis once people knew him through his songs, films and shows; keeping silent is no way for an upcoming act to get into the public eye.

A young Bryan Adams was very keen to let the press and radio programmers know he had arrived as a happening artist, and once or twice he even suggested headlines which would make good copy for his story.[5] Bryan's key ploy was to say that he was a regular guy. The epithet was not an invention of the press, but something that Adams' regularly labelled himself.[6] And certainly, the evidence suggested, in a strange kind of way, that he really was a regular guy, albeit with middle-class roots. He kept his own name, had an almost disappointing lack of pretension and broached no project, it seemed, beyond simply having a good tine and perhaps getting famous into the bargain. He also dressed down and along the way had somehow subtly picked up trappings as an honest rocker - a common man made good - a hero from straight out of everyday life. The implication was that perhaps he had been a busker, a street musician, unchanged by his newly found fame, unmoved from his goal of claiming a little corner of rock'n'roll for himself. Accordingly, his act wasn't theatre, artifice, pure escapism or Vegas-style show business glitz.

Chapter 4

Everything was orientated toward saying that standing on stage was a guy who just the other day could have pumped gas for us, gone out with our sister, stacked supermarket shelves, fixed our car, or done any number of run-of-the-mill activities. Adams' ability to rock glamorized everyday life. Put more simply, because audiences knew that Bryan was the kid next door, when he delivered a storming set in front of their very eyes, they knew it was because he had to rock out as a way to escape from the everyday world that everyone shared. Dressing down was therefore a way to convert the concert hall into the school yard, teenager's bedroom, the gas station at coffee break time, or another ordinary place where people could find a space to escape the treadmill of others telling them what to do. It became a setting for urgent pleasures shared in desperation.

The attitude was there in the way that Adams' stage set drew upon songs by acts from times past. As he once said, technically he was a hack, and he was - as most rockers are.[7] Bryan was influenced by the music of all sorts of people in the 1960s and 1970s: he scoured the efforts of anybody who actually attained musical fame to unlock their secrets. For his own show however, Adams restricted cover versions almost entirely to groups such as The Beatles and early rockers like Eddy Cochran. Significantly, returning to the Fab Four's songs was a way to evoke their early values, as the Liverpudlians who had elevated being ordinary - and therefore having a right to speak for ordinary people - to an art form.

On top of the spartan, good times attitude was an almost imperceptible edge of resistance. A very slight and subtle language of rock'n'roll defiance was deployed to put an edge on Adams image, as a way to inflect him and market what was already there: the ordinary guy, his stage show and, in the eye of the storm, his music. To his widest catchment of fans, Bryan Adams was known through the videos for *Reckless*. He was that guy singing in the fallen leaves, grappling with on-stage alienation in 'Heaven', and confusing the police in a rat run of industrial buildings on the video for 'Summer of '69': at some times, a sensitive nice guy, but at others a cheeky rebel. A&M knew that Adams' image as a bad-boy rocker was what sold, because in 1986 they re-released *Cuts Like A Knife* in the UK with a particular new sleeve. On the colour cover shot Bryan was pictured looking virtually the same as he had on *Reckless*, complete with his leather jacket on and the collar turned up. Even if it was the label's marketing men who threw out the mack jacket and got Adams to combine leather and an angst ridden stare, it was Bryan himself who chose the old, robust rock'n'roll covers for his band. For Adams, tunes from the '50s came charged with all the energy that could rift open a gap between teens and their parents, and could use sexuality as the means to define a generation by doing something as simple as dancing.

The strange thing was that there was, if we can begin to cut away the hype, a slight air of nonchalance to the real Bryan Adams, a bravado which came through on many occasions. The cocky kid-next-door moniker was not just a marketing technique, but an attitude which kept him at the centre of attention. He jibed Margaret Trudea, the wayward spouse of Canada's one time president, for her fling with The Stones. He also told off the benign but nauseous entrepreneur Richard Branson on broadcast television. Adams was a man of few words, but they were plain and direct. He never traded in unwarranted respect or hid behind diplomacy.

A more direct example of Bryan's flippancy was when he took a sky dive with a trained parachutist over Memphis in June 1985. For a few heart-stopping moments the parachute cable tangled round the men as they plummeted downwards. It could have been the end of the new star's life or career, or at least the start of a phase in hospital. Luckily the situation was soon righted and when the two men finally touched down, Adams just dusted himself off and said "Let's have a beer."[8] It would be logical to suspect that Adams' attitude didn't arise really because he was born an uncaring jerk, but because, in the face of intense pressure and criticism, sometimes the only sane route is not to care. With some relatively barren years on the road behind him - at one stage the singer was $100,000 in debt to his own manager – Adams confessed "I've learned to believe in myself when other people didn't want to."[9] Yet Bryan would not allow himself to be too careless when fame at last came his way, since he needed its sustenance. Perhaps Adams knew that for many who had gone before him, fame was like candyfloss: it looked nice and was sweet in your mouth, but as soon as you tasted it, it was gone.

Adams' primary aim was acceptance and longevity as a singer, rather than condemnation as a rebel: in a sense he had to limit himself. His advantage was that he had an image which worked in its own absence, since he could be whatever you wanted him to be. What was important was the way that his persona set eventual limits on what role he could conceivably be interpreted as playing within the fantasies of his fans. For example, he was too honest to be a pickpocket, not pious enough to be a priest and not selfish enough to be hustling down on Wall Street.

Correspondingly, Adams had set limits on how he could be apprehended as a star. He was too sane to get involved with drug abuse or self-mutilation, and too disciplined to be caught choking his guitar like it was a wayward farm animal. He occasionally warned boisterous fans in the front rows not to push forward; a far cry from some of the early rockers who left riots in their wake because their music got the kids so worked-up.

This brings us to the question of how Bryan Adams - his music and image, as a slightly defiant regular guy - could be

appropriated by his fans. Adams' middle class background
formed a typical section of his press biographies, but it seemed
to have no effect on his popularity.[10] That's nothing unusual:
many fans know, but do not care, that rockers are not what they
seem. The question is why young middle class audiences had felt
a need for somebody with Adams' kind of image.

Rock'n'roll is a medium that summons up a space of dreams in
which, as fans, we escape from the mundane routine of daily life.
It is a mythical environment - a land of opportunity - full of
heroes, missionaries, royalty, mercenaries, legends and leaders of
the people. It even contains a messiah or two, but it's also a
wasteland teeming with miscreants, mutants, lowlifes and
tattooed reprobates. Even if some of them claim an urge to say
what they have to (whether we like it or not) rock's alumni offer
themselves up for our scrutiny and remain successful only
through recognition from an audience. What fans are looking for
is someone different enough to do things that they might never
get to do, but not so outlandish that no one can associate with
them. As a result, rock stars are granted powers to speak the
unspoken, right relationships, pull followers together into
communities of common feeling, and do the things of which
your parents would not approve.

If musicians provide fans with a beat to dance to, it is rock stars
who on our behalf vicariously explore the lives that we can't lead.
What many admire is their sense of mission, the idea that we can
dance to their music but at the same time it builds towards other
goals. Once stars show up, we suss them out, commune with
them, assess them, and finally expect of them. Because a song is
a way to vent private feelings in public places and a way to
channel community, sometimes we let them speak for us. Above
all, what fans want from their idols is something they can identify
with, be that utterly escapist or unbelievably relevant. The most

fundamental rule is that we take the stars - like them, hate them or don't care - as we find them.

With the growing acceptance of Bryan Adams, focusing critical attention upon him, the wall of silence which Bruce Allen advocated (following the career of Elvis) continued to stay up. However, Adams' standoff with the press was conveniently broken when he had new material to promote. Also if the singer became furious about something, he would tell the papers and Allen could do little about it. The policy - creating a space in which the performer could be missed by his audience - was advantageous because Adams was not cornered into talking trivia or wasting words in other ways. Because the public did not know or see Bryan Adams offstage or outside of the recording studio, although the idea may have been to focus on his act, the natural compunction of people was to fill in the blanks themselves.

Adams was neutral enough to be the receptacle of others' fantasies. Since his background and interests were unwritten, going on the few clues they had, listeners could write in their own scripts with only their imagination as a guide. Bryan's fans were mostly middle class kids, so it was important that their mythical landscape was working class, as long as it was mythical in the sense of being shorn of all the downside of that existence. Perhaps what Adams centrally suggested was that, with old fashioned hard work - after all in his act he essentially performed a service - even the most regular of people could attain a phenomenal level of success. The result was almost guaranteed Harlequin rock romance.

Guys who came just to rock could also envisage other roles for Adams, since he was one of them - one of the lads - but also a leader who marshalled his band like a gang behind him. He always worked in unison with them to further his aims. In essence, while he was an ordinary person, at the same time he could do things that they couldn't do, but given the extreme demands of the moment, they might have hoped to achieve. Even top hard rockers were impressed with the way that Adams could glide with ease between their songs and his intimate ballads.

Bryan also had more than a few female fans since mythically he was a nice guy and more. Female and gay fans gave their dreams about Adams a sexual and/or relationship orientated component, as his natural, unposed masculinity suggested certain qualities.[11] He was more concerned about his relationship than how he looked in the mirror. He was plain enough to take you home to mum but, when you were out of her sight, was also capable of behaving in ways that she wouldn't have approved - although you most certainly would. He was sane enough not to be an embarrassment at the wrong moment, but mad enough to have a laugh when the time was right. He was tough enough to stick up for you, but sensible enough to avoid an unwarranted fight. He was extraordinarily talented but modest to a fault, and, above all, a hard working guy: a provider, a model citizen and someone who would have made a good patriot accordingly. These qualities worked their magic. In 1982 readers of the Canadian magazine *Musical Express* had already voted him the sexiest performer of the year, while the women's magazine *Chatelaine* later put him forward as one of the country's top ten sexiest men. Then there was the wide speculation suggesting he'd had a fling with Tina Turner. All this attention was in spite of the fact that Adams never indulged in the prurient onstage exploits of, say, Prince.

Like the fans, all the press had to go on was *what they could see*: some guy raising the roof with nothing but his music, unkempt blond hair and a guileless stare. He was a delinquent who could work a building better than anyone else in the business, but his low-key approach meant that, in order to make good copy, press reporters had to play upon elements of his visual identity.[12]

Alternatively, there was always Adams' relatively novel citizenship to fall back on. The Canadian press compared him to other national luminaries, while the British caught on to his Canadian 'hoser' image and went in for some light-hearted stereotyping.[13]

If Adams was seen as a regular Canadian by commentators based abroad, another way journalists chose to interpret him was by looking through the lens of rock history. One reaction was a sense of novelty, since, despite it all, Bryan had remained a regular guy. He bought his own airline tickets and was even accosted by a security guard at one of his own gigs because he looked and acted so normal. This kind of shock of the obvious could only happen after the critics had suffered an assorted parade of egocentric maestros, individuals who went overboard to live the myth of the rock'n'roll lifestyle. Traditionally such people used their new-found wealth for displays that showed fans they were leading lives in the fast lane. They led lives of excess that ordinary folk couldn't live, but might want to if they had the money.

Realistically, the stress of sudden fame had a power to create addicts and overdose victims. What Bryan Adams showed was that someone with ambition could play rock, work hard and find real fame, all without the excess. His uncanny normality therefore appeared unusual because, outside the music, he was not doing what was expected of a rocker. Yet the idea of Bryan Adams as someone unusually normal had limited mileage because people in touch with the rock business knew that its extremists had died long ago, gone crazy, sobered up, or run themselves down.

The 1980s was a decade when record labels made the acts pay their own expenses. It meant that you could be famous without being rich. Upcoming stars often kept their day jobs longer than anyone hoped. When Adams started to gain attention, an army of music scribes began to scrutinize his songs, to suss out his image, and to look for comparisons in order to situate him for listeners on a map of the rock'n'roll landscape. As far as the songs went, the general opinion was that the material was derivative and recycled: everyone's favourite old influences were felt to be there in the mix, but nobody could put their finger on exactly what had been taken on board. The effect was to excite younger ones and bemuse older ones. His broken, low register vocals - once described as a voice that needed a shave - lured journalists into making comparisons with everyone and anyone. Even though many of Adams inspirations (acts he covered on stage, said he liked, or saw in his youth) were British, the Canadian rocker was usually compared to American artists.

Comparisons between Bryan Adams and Other Acts [14]

Nationality of Acts	No of Comparisons[15]	No of Influences
American	34 with 10 acts	3 acts
British	11 with 5 acts	7 acts
Australian	1 act (AC/DC)	1 act (AC/DC)
Canadian	1 act (Corey Hart)	

With an uncanny frequency, Bruce Springsteen became the name that was suggested alongside Adams, partly because Adams' success followed in the wake of the path forged by Springsteen's *Born in the USA* album and tour.

Springsteen had been known for a long time as rock's messiah; a man who exercised an almost magical grip over awestruck fans and writers. With his latest album, the Boss turned to rock anthems and unlimited marketing in the bid to get his message across. *Born In The USA*, which had been mixed by Bob

Chapter 4

Clearmountain just before *Reckless,* thus set the standards for anthemic 1980's rock. In Springsteen's wake just about anyone who came along and dressed down to hammer chords from their Stratocaster would have been viewed through a distinctly New Jerseyan perspective. The result was that writers grappled with Adams. Because he *wasn't* the Boss, the comparisons were at arm's length. As a way to cope with the situation, an arsenal of prefixes was pulled off the shelf: Adams was considered as something of a "road company", "junior" or "bargain basement" Springsteen.

Certainly Adams had some things in common with the Boss: both men took up their guitars as personal weapons to provide spartan but energetic stage spectacles, and each did everything they could to suggest that fame had not changed them. They shared a way of dressing down for live shows in plain tee shirts and jeans which marked them out as regular guys.[16] The style was not new, since it was sported by earlier Canadian rockers like Neil Young and The Guess Who. Yet by the 1980s it had also become a recurrent theme outside the world of popular music. For example, back in the early 1970s dirt and democracy became chic, and middle class Canadians dressed in manual work clothes.[17] Springsteen made the style popular once more to associate himself with working class Americans.

Springsteen's down-at-heel dress sense and the puritanical minimalism of his live shows were both moves calculated to say that fame had not changed him, since he still remembered and allied himself to his roots - roots that were on the same stratum as the underdogs of America. His message was that the things which Americans are told to hold dear (such as blind patriotism and the American dream) need questioning in light of the predicament of poorer people. Springsteen picked up his guitar like a man called to arms. It was a "tool to open doors", a way to change the world and simultaneously have a good time, to break out politically and feel good about doing so.[18] On an endless journey - or perhaps struggle - towards fulfilling his project, he had explored all sorts of emotions and told many a dark tale on the way. There was the escapist resistance of 'Born To Run,' the nostalgic despondency of 'The River,' all the bleakness of 'Nebraska' and the submerged irony of 'Born In The USA.' Yet the way he conveyed his message was through songs that simultaneously reinvested everyday life with hope.

In terms of music, style and project, the two regular guys of rock'n'roll were subtly different. Adams had no saxophonist like Clarence Clemons to provide the over-paced element to his sound and, since his songs were more romantic and parochial, he needed none of the teeth-gritting angst or coldness which Springsteen could summon up to cope with the wider world. Adams had not cultivated his image as a regular guy for any political purpose, but that very fact meant that he had encountered disapproval from those who thought rock should be about *more* than how you got on with your girlfriend.

Even if they didn't make it explicit, more seasoned journalists often felt awkward because they now saw someone hijacking the regular guy archetype and taking it in a new, conservative direction. Adams was given a roasting by some critics whenever they got an opportunity, often in proportion to his new found popularity. The case against Bryan claimed that his music was derivative and that themes were recycled, that he was an opportunist who talked in clichés and had nothing of substance to say. However, while Adams appeared guilty on some of those counts, it was really a matter of perspective. Bryan was certainly a populist. As he once suggested: "The difference between me and the critics is that I don't think being commercial is a bad thing; that's just giving your audience what they want."[19] Speaking in clichés was a way to tap into a common vocabulary that the singer and his fans could share, and it was difficult to describe him as Mr. Boring when he could also deliver rock'n'roll at a voltage high enough to drive his fans wild.

The amazing thing was that the same scribes who criticized Adams never dismissed Springsteen's venture into populism as the farce that it sometimes was. *Born In The USA* elevated the scale of his act into spectacle, politically pacifying, rather than activating his spectators. His success was latched onto in a way that detracted from - and even inverted - his message: he was apprehended as a regular guy being successful and thus proving the American Dream, as a patriotic American and as a sex symbol. Attention was focused upon the man himself rather than those to whom he pointed.[20] In short, although they arrived from different positions, because they had a similar approach, Springsteen and Adams had often been tackled in the same way. If the Boss was old enough to know better, Bryan was naive enough to get caught up with what his critics had to say.

The paradox of the star that "had no image" was complete, since no image *was* the image that he had. By acting as a regular guy, Adams could be taken, within reason, as whatever fans wanted him to be. If they chose to embrace him on a personal level, it was the press who mistook him as a representative leader of men. Most real regular guys would have just been content to get wealthy, and show it in perhaps the ways that were upheld as the rock'n'roll lifestyle. As a performer who was sensitive about his peers and press, Bryan Adams went beyond that. In order to avoid being written off as a lightweight, he felt compelled to step into the realm of politics. It was one ball game for which he had not prepared.

---

[1] *Saturday Night* (v.107/9, 11/92, p.86).

[2] *Canadian Musician* (v.7/5, 5/10/85, p.47).

[3] *Montreal Gazette* (10/1/85, p.D).

[4] *Maclean's* magazine (v.94/47, 23/11/81, p.50).

[5] For example "Bryan Adams Goes for the Throat" (*Winnipeg Free Press* 12/5/82, p.28).

[6] "He's a regular guy, he insists" (Kamin, 1985, p.1).

[7] *Maclean's* magazine (v.94/47, 23/11/81, p.50).

[8] *Maclean's* magazine (5/8/85, p.55).

[9] *Globe and Mail* (25/6/83, p.25).

[10] See the *Toronto Star* (25/2/92, p.A1), and *Saturday Night* (v.107/9, 1992, p.82).

[11] See *Chatelaine* (v.58/10, 1985, p.8), or an article by a gay reviewer in *Creem* (v.19/2, 10/87, p.49) who asked "Isn't sex appeal most powerful when it comes across naturally and spontaneously?"

[12] They stressed the dynamism of his live shows as work sessions (*Life & Times* 21/7/92, p.2; *Globe and Mail* 12/2/92, p.E2); giving him manual occupations to suit the occasion, such as Okanagan fruit picker (*Vancouver Sun* 8/9/92, p.C1); exploring his

masculinity as a sex symbol or as a mark of his ordinariness like a roguish boy next door (*Rolling Stone* 10/9/87, p.42).

[13] 'Hoser' is a term used for dumb, macho, regular Canadian guys. When Adams was compared to Canadians they were usually national figures rather than musicians. For example at least three times he has been compared to hockey star Wayne Gretzky (*Vancouver Sun* 5/10/85, p.A1; *Maclean's* v.100/27, 1987, p.32; Globe and Mail 13/9/92, p.C1). Associations made in Britain were with Canadian stereotypes such as the bar circuit. For example "I can't quite make out what he's advertising, Canadian lager perhaps?" (*Melody Maker* v.62/14, 1988, p.22). "It was quite possible to imagine oneself in a sawdust-floored tavern watching the Adams group perform under a neon sign advertising Labatts beer." (*Life & Times* 21/7/92, p.2). Also, upon learning that Adams had recorded an album in his Vancouver house, one reporter suggested his next was to be "recorded with the assistance of a pack of huskies and a squad of mounties" (*Melody Maker* v.62/15, 1987, p.17).

[14] This table is based on a non-exhaustive but extensive, search of the *Canadian Musician, Chatelaine, The Globe and Mail, Maclean', Melody Maker, Music Scene, New York Times, Rolling Stone, Saturday Night, Spin, The Toronto Star, The Times,* and *Variety.*

[15] Separate figures are given for the total number of comparisons made between Adams and acts from a particular country, and also the number of acts from each country with whom he was compared. For example, Adams was compared to 10 American acts, but because writers collectively compared him to many of these acts more than once, he was compared to American artists a collective total of 34 times. In that particular case, he was

compared to Springsteen 17 times, and the remaining 17 comparisons were distributed between 9 other artists.

[16] Adams manufactured this image for himself. He demonstrated it in different ways which became part of his story. These included everything down to a lack of long guitar solos in his songs (*Guitar Player* v.21, 1987, p.26). While not unusual in themselves, such elements became relevant as things not associated with rock stars.

[17] *Maclean's* magazine (v.84/5, 1971, p.41; v.84/6, 1971, p.54; v.85/3, 1972, p.32).

[18] *Maclean's* magazine (v.91/32, 18/12/78, p.5).

[19] *Vancouver Sun* (31/8/85, p.D4).

[20] *Newsweek* (13/4/87, p.74).

5

Into The Fire: Social Causes

Rock'n'roll realizes that its songs function within life more than any previous art historically ever has.
- Richard Meltzer (1970)[1]

It's better to remember that we're pop musicians, not politicians and that line should never be crossed.
- Bryan Adams (1987)[2]

With the huge success of *Reckless*, there were to be no deadlines for the next album. Bryan Adams had enough money in the bank to sit back a little and take stock. A few years earlier Adams' primary goal was to rock out and find gratification in being famous, just like his own musical idols had done before him. It was a burning ambition for which he would have done anything, including signing a $1 contract with A&M, and pestering an indifferent Bruce Allen.

Adams' early musical efforts were unfocused and indicated that he was a man of talent who was trying whatever avenue he could; one might even say an opportunist. Now, in the wake of a bestselling album, he was known to the public as a slightly naughty but hard working rocker whose guitar never left his hands. In some quarters he was seen as an unassuming sex symbol too. Yet, despite his success, Adams was in a cleft stick. On one hand, Bruce Allen's dream of shaping his act to cater to the baby boomers had not really come to pass. On the other, veteran critics were using Adams' young audience to indicate he was a teeny bopper champion - a junior Springsteen – and a lightweight with nothing important to say. Perhaps unwisely, he read his own press and it hurt. Although Adams was no diplomat, he had always been very peer conscious. After the other rock and pop stars who had stormed the charts in the 1980s became committed to social causes, Adams became interested in lending his new-found weight to such efforts. Cautiously, Bryan began to demonstrate his concerns about (non-partisan) political issues.

Adams was not altering his morals to suit his market - for example he had been a committed member of the Vancouver-based organization Greenpeace for years - but now he wanted to show another side of his character. It was a chance to rebuff his critics, gain peer approval from other stars, and perhaps secure an older, more thoughtful audience.

Bryan had a lot to gain. His biggest asset was that he had already proved himself a powerful communicator. As a popular performer he was valuable to anyone who wished to tell a young audience about things. Moreover, the man with the broken voice had an ability to charge songs with a jaded intensity which would be excellent for conveying whatever issues he chose to air. Bryan had a potential like that of the old blues men who, by bemoaning their individual circumstances, reflected a wider oppression.

Since Adams had already been greeted as a 'regular guy' by his fans, Bryan would, by showing his political concerns from the heart of the spectacle, imply that regular guys everywhere might share a similar sense of morality and willingness to try and change the world. One performer who had already managed to reflect a wider oppression was Bruce Springsteen. The Boss always had an edge of political concern which propelled his songs, and to his credit he could look unflinchingly at the darker side of American life. The difference between Adams and Springsteen was that when the Boss sang about relationships it was almost as if they were the last bastion of resistance against an otherwise miserable environment ruled by wider forces like the economy. Adams' songs were heart-breaking dramas with a more parochial focus. His listeners were rarely given a glimpse of the world beyond each song's immediate crisis of young love.

As someone who became famous for pure entertainment, the Groover from Vancouver faced new difficulties when he began using his fame for other ends. Adams had to face new questions of hypocrisy, ulterior motives and, of course, the possibility of losing more fans than he would gain. To express social causes more publicly was, then, a brave step which Adams felt he had to take, and as the 1980s ran their course he began to do so.

To assess Adams' new direction, it is important to understand the wider structures of feeling that surrounded rock in the mid-1980s. People who argue that rock and politics have parted company since the 1970s have tended to base their positions only on the lyrics to most current songs.[3] Yet in the 1980s, whether we look at protest songs played on nostalgic radio formats, old hits used in advertising or seemingly apolitical songs played at benefit gigs, changing the context of popular songs was one of the main ways that they were used politically.[4]

Crucially, artists exercise a degree of moral control over their songs by preventing their use for undesirable causes and/or by promoting desirable interpretations. For example, as the owner of copyright, a songwriter can determine whether his or her work will be broadcast, but broadcasting is just one instance where artists have some control over the context in which their work gets heard. There are many others. Artists are still central to the politics of rock, because they hold the power to prevent or allow songs to be put into certain contexts. Ultimately it is they who decide whether to use the appeal of their songs for particular ends.

Adams' appearance at Live Aid in 1985 showed 1.5 billion viewers that although he could party, Bryan was committed to much more, and could bring the full force of having a good time to bear on consciousness-raising activities. In fact, due to his immense popularity (save for an expatriated Neil Young) Adams was the only Canadian to play at the internationally-staged event.

So far, so good: the Canadian singer had put his popularity with the rock audience into a worthy context and gained exposure in the process. Similarly the 'Tears Are Not Enough' session had been a successful fund-raising exercise and also an eye-opener that showed Adams and Vallance what might be done by dint of their own efforts. If 1985 was the year in which Bryan coasted on the euphoria surrounding *Reckless*, the next year was a time for him to switch track.

For much of 1986 Canada's premier rocker was off the road. He spent time at home with Vicki Russell, wrote songs with Jim

Vallance, pruned rose bushes in his garden and retreated into the woods. After his endearing single, Adams had become a firm favourite with Lady Diana, so he went over to England for a Royal Command performance at a Prince's Trust benefit gig. He played for the Royal couple again as part of Expo '86 in Vancouver and, in line with his new style, Adams gave all of the $100,000 he earned for the show away to charity.

Following Amnesty International's previous caravan venture, Bryan also took part in their Conspiracy Of Hope tour. Politically it was a step beyond Live Aid. The idea was not to pool the forces of popular music into a transitory spectacle, but instead to demonstrate pop acts as living examples who would suggest to fans that it was important to commit themselves in a similar way.

The tour went to six cities across North America and saw Amnesty's membership base rocket accordingly. Adams was amongst a considerably older musical cohort, most of whom had become famous in the New Wave of the early '80s or before. He got a chance to walk the same stage as luminaries like Sting, Peter Gabriel and U2. While it must have felt awkward going on stage to sing a song like 'Kids Wanna Rock' between two protest numbers - something out of tune with what the audience expected - that was not the reason Adams started writing less neutral material. He and Vallance had written all the socially-conscious songs that were to appear on the next album *before* the Amnesty tour.

As Adams got publicly involved with even more issues, he demonstrated a more active sense of concern. Towards the middle of 1986 he wrote in to the *Vancouver Province* to complain about the USS Constellation and its 8 warships stationed in English Bay, because, ironically, they were an American invasion of protective force in a nuclear free zone. By revealing his credentials as a pacifist, Adams bucked the family tradition and did it in the place where he meant more to fans than just another hero - his hometown. The letter sparked vigorous debate for a while as local fans exchanged salvoes across the letters pages of the newspaper.

Despite such controversy, Adams was still seen as enviable property by backers in the music industry. That year he was voted the 6th hottest act in the world by an American panel of music industry experts. Also Bryan was approached once again by Hollywood, this time to contribute a song to the Tom Cruise film 'Top Gun.' His manager viewed the offer as a smart business move, but Adams saw the film's rushes after laying down 'Only The Strong Survive' with Jim Vallance and decided that he wanted to have nothing to do with such a glorification of war. With a policy of avoiding personal administration or getting in the way of his act's art, Bruce Allen had to watch the opportunity slip away. The film became immensely successful while Adams kept his songs solely for the next album.

Although Allen was probably frustrated by the episode, as usual he had other things in which to dabble. In 1986 Bruce added the popular Canadian classical guitarist Lyonna Boyd to his roster. Also Jim Vallance remained active, winning a Juno for his writing efforts which, unlike the previous two years, he did not have to share with Bryan Adams. While those two associates showed they could exist without Bryan, the public was eagerly waiting on more songs from Adams as the next year began. In mid-March, A&M could at last provide fresh material, and made every effort to push Bryan's new LP, giving it a simultaneous release in 45 different countries. In Canada alone the new Adams / Vallance album, *Into The Fire*, shipped over 430,000 units before it even hit the racks.

The line-up for the new album consisted of all the regulars, but there was a slight hint that Adams was looking for a polished English pop sound. In fact, he wanted to bring in Chris Hughes, the producer of Tears For Fears' 1985 album *Songs From The Big Chair*. In the end Ian Stanley - their keyboard player - guested on a few tracks, but there was no Lou Gramm: the Foreigner veteran who contributed an American edge to the last two LPs. Also the songs were recorded in Bryan's house for a change of scene, and, in the absence of Hughes, Adams and Clearmountain once again shared production duties. North of False Creek, over in West Vancouver, Adams set up a $150,000 recording studio in his basement with a 48 track recorder and two-way Sony Camera link to elsewhere in the house. It made a change from booking time at the busy Little Mountain Sound. Although the masters finally got mixed by Clearmountain over in England, on the LP sleeve Bryan's home studio was credited as Cliffhanger Studios.

While A&M didn't have to pay so much for studio time, they actually spent a staggering $250,000 putting the new effort into the public arena with a particularly extensive marketing campaign. Fifty top media people were flown to a respectable Toronto hotel for an LP release dinner party. The event was attended by PROCAN's president Jan Matjchek who then proudly reported to Canadian songwriters that the new music was not only a step forward for Adams, but it showed the heights to which a Canadian could go.[5]

In fact, there was a general sense that Adams had arrived as an artist and could now call the shots. Officials at A&M saw the LP as a sign that Bryan was maturing as an artist - looking for a new direction - and they treated him accordingly. He had been given room to renegotiate his contract with the label for a third time, so he could take a slightly larger cut from the sale of each unit. Also, as with *Cuts Like A Knife* but not *Reckless*, the songs were copyrighted to Adams Communications, Inc., a company which

Chapter 5

Bryan established to accumulate and invest his profits, run routinely by his mother. Through that channel, more money went Adams' way.

The new album cover showed Bryan caught against a bleak expanse of open water (False Creek) in front of industrial port land. He wore a white shirt with the top button done up, adding an air of respectability underneath his trademark leather jacket. The shirt would have been well suited to a young Bono, or even an old Bill Wyman: it was a sober way for one musician to show to others that he was financially wealthy now because his music was popular. To suit the occasion, a subtle reorientation of Adams' rocker image was taking place.

However, despite the respect of A&M, the new album appeared to be a kind of lame return to the type of material on *Cuts Like A Knife*, and in places worse. Using the working title of *Against The Grain*, Adams and company had produced a distinctly cold and unfocussed collection. Perhaps the best tracks were the more standard rock fare: 'Heat of The Night' and 'Hearts on Fire.' A&M cleverly avoided the release of the less exciting social issue-orientated material as singles. Instead they promoted 'Heat of The Night' as the first cassette single in Canada. It was a case of using a popular performer to spearhead new ways of tapping the market.

The more politicized songs went off in all directions. On an autobiographical piece about the tough decisions he made to follow the new path called 'Into The Fire', Adams sounded down in the mouth. It was almost as if he didn't want to be there. Even on the album cover, Vancouver's top act could not look us in the eye. 'Another Day' was a particular low point: lyrically the song was Adams' portrayal of the realities of life on the welfare line, but musically it was just glib blues. Both the anguish and irony of the whole situation were missed; a sign of a performer out of touch with his subject matter. A mixed bag of songs on the album also suggested the same point: 'Remembrance Day' was from the position of a World War One soldier (inspired by one of Vallance's forebears), while another number was from the viewpoint of an Indian chief. As a rocker, Bryan Adams had mustered a considerable trace of authenticity; it was expecting too much of him to act out all these other roles.

Moreover, Adams had bought a distinctly middle class sensibility to his work: guilt. To suddenly feel guilty about everybody else's injustices was not the way that working class heroes would have reacted, and the fans knew it, so Bryan was in a difficult spot. Young fans found the new material irrelevant to their lives and would probably have preferred more good-timing (as in a *Reckless II*) or even a more escapist approach. Reviewers said Adams new work was unprofound and at least one suggested that he should have put more of himself into the writing. Some more discerning audience segments found the material vague, and in part still musically-oriented to regular fans: one critic for the *Village Voice* counted 56 clichés in the new album. Although the initial reaction to *Into The Fire* was so disappointing, Adams remained convinced of his ability to turn tour audiences into loyal customers for his records. Undaunted, he prepared to hit the road again.

In the spring of 1987 Bryan played another Prince's Trust benefit gig but, by June, Bruce Allen noticed press interest in his boy was low compared with other artists. As a result he organised a champagne party in New York's Landmark Tavern, at the same time Adams played the city. The festivities did not stop there. Joined offstage occasionally by Vicki Russell, Adams did 150 dates to promote his new album across Europe, Canada, the US and Australia in front of a total of around 1.5 million fans. July began with Bryan doing a special Canada Day gig in Toronto, while he planned to participate in a multiple location concert for Greenpeace called Rock The World in early September. In October, Adams earned $75,000 for a single concert in front of his fans in Toronto. By early December, after 9 months on the road, he came home. A reasonable $45 million gross in ticket sales had accrued from the whole venture. Furthermore Bruce Allen engineered a favourable system for Adams' concert merchandising, just as he had done with Loverboy, so that the star got one third of the $15 million gross profits made on his tour from such activity.

The tour profits were insignificant compared to the potential money Adams could have made by producing a more popular album. The initial kick given to the LP by A&M had helped: it had got to number 1 in Canada and eventually went triple platinum. In the USA, since Adams had a loyal fan base it had gone platinum in 4 months. As things panned out, however, it became clear that compared to *Reckless*, the new LP's sales figures showed that by moving into an area for which he was not known Adams had lost 65% (6 million) of his previous customers. For a smaller artist it might have been curtains, but Bryan Adams and his team had enough money now to roll with the punches. Each single that stormed the American charts bought home at least $200,000 in royalty cheques for Adams and Vallance. Also Bruce Allen had been a multi-millionaire for quite a few years on his cut of the profits of BTO, Loverboy and Adams. In 1988, ever the opinionated businessman, Allen decided to branch out once more and started a label called Penta Records.

With all the revenue from his album sales, tours, merchandise, royalties and the songs he sold to other acts, Bryan Adams had amassed a fortune out of all proportion with his image as one of the common people. In fact, by 1988 it was estimated that he had a net worth of around $35 million - which included at least

$8 million from radio royalties alone - much of it handled by the Adams Communication Corporation. Although fame had always been a key part of his project, it is unlikely that Adams ever set out to milk the system like Loverboy had done and to retire quickly and comfortably. After all, he had not produced an obvious immediate sequel to *Reckless* and had instead made a different album on his own terms. But being conscious of what others thought of him, Bryan realized that to work again in the same way would probably return him to the minor leagues. His wealth gave him more time to reflect on his own mistakes and make sure that next time he would deliver something really excellent.

In the meantime, Adams could not shake his road fever. In 1988 he was back out on tour. He did a free gig in Calgary in January for athletes in the Winter Olympics. He then went back over to Europe for a tour which included a date behind the iron curtain, in Budapest, two sold-out shows in Zurich, and some concerts in the capital cities of Scandinavia. In France, audiences remained unimpressed, probably because Bryan reminded them too much of Bruce Springsteen. Despite his dedication to the road, Adams was soon enough embroiled in even more political debate.

In November the Ottawa Defence Department decided to use 'Remembrance Day' as the theme for a $55,000 video which showed archival footage of soldiers in action, mixed with ranks of teens standing to attention. The idea was to talk to those too young to remember the world wars in a language that they could understand. Adams consented, because he said that the project, like his song, did not glamorize war in any way. The harrowing result of ODD's vision and its soundtrack song was sent out to a number of Canadian Schools. 1,800 legion halls were also offered copies, but initially they refused because they had heard that it contained a rock score. It seemed that rock music still had bad connotations for some old soldiers. What was odd, though, was that Bryan Adams was willing to align himself with authorities who stockpiled arms in his effort to say that war was a nasty and regrettable experience – the same authorities in effect whom Bryan's father had worked for, although he had eventually retired to live on Vancouver Island. If the Adams' legend had initially been fuelled by stories about Conrad's stance as an opera fanatic who winced at his son's interest in rock, now it was no longer so important. Bryan Adams had now resolved his differences with his father. Conrad even attended one of his son's concerts, before walking out with the fear that he might go deaf.

Bryan's willingness to donate his song to the Defence Department showed he was willing to compromise for his causes, but it also indicated that he still considered them important. Bruce Allen's suggestion that Adams should stay silent had largely been followed by his act. As a result, the late 1980s became a time during which Bryan was known alternately for his songs and vociferous complaints about particular political issues: the public never got to see all sides of the singer. In fact, now it was almost as if a man *without an image in a way* had become defined by the array of struggles with which he associated. Late in 1989, he stepped into the fray again to support another cause: building conservation.

As a kid who grew up in various European cities, Adams had seen the way that old buildings can give particular places their characteristic flavour. Life on the road in Europe was a constant reminder, but back in Canada urban policies helped make the feel of cities very different. Vancouver was seen by developers, in line with its buoyant economy and lively cosmopolitan atmosphere, as a place for creating new building projects. While the city was barely a century old, periodic redevelopments were constantly cutting down old landmarks. In particular a series of 1930s Art Deco buildings were being demolished. The Georgia medical and dental building was a much loved example that had just sadly been knocked down.

Adams swung into action to protest about the aesthetic restructuring of his home city. An interview in the *Vancouver Sun* was arranged as a public forum for him to put his case. He also sent a letter to the city's mayor, suggesting that building owners should be offered tax breaks to put them off making quick-buck sales to eager developers. Denny Boyd interviewed Bryan for a Canadian architectural journal, where the concerned rocker explained, "I'll be 45 someday and I'll be looking at a city I don't recognize. I feel I have to protest."[6] Boyd said that he had initially underestimated Adams' conviction, but he ended up on the other side of the fence attesting that the singer's strength of feeling was real. Certainly, the Vancouver rocker had been moved by what he saw going on, but rather than playing benefit gigs in aid of building conservation, Bryan decided to include a song on his next album to publicize the issue. Also, instead of replacing an old building by constructing something new, in Gastown Adams bought a historic building himself for the purpose of converting it into a new studio. He practiced what he preached.

Perhaps to centre the debate entirely on Adams' degree of conviction was to ignore what was really happening. The whole incident was rather like the controversy over Prince Charles's comments about the face of London. In both cases it was a matter of people who were famous for other reasons levering their celebrity to speak out about things that they felt were especially important. Adams had a name that could guarantee press attention. He had a privileged voice that could set debates rolling to explore his own protest agenda. The practicality of the situation (jobs created, people sheltered, etc.) was subsumed under aesthetic judgments. Seemingly, it did not matter that Bryan was not a qualified housing expert or architect. What mattered was his ability to represent the thoughts of a mythical 'guy from the street'. The urban environment debate showed that Bryan Adams, now just into his thirties, could pick political fights of his own accord and rally the Canadian public behind him. It was a sign of what was to follow.

---

[1] Taken from Meltzer's book *The Aesthetics of Rock* (1987, p.84).

[2] *Canadian Musician* (v.9/4, 8/87, p.49).

[3] This does not mean that there were no acts still writing politicized songs outside genres such as rap and folk. In fact, politicized acts as diverse as Sting, Billy Bragg and REM remained popular. Furthermore, songs that seem ambiguous can still become significant in particular contexts. While remaining open to interpretation on record, many lyrics have a lot of potential to raise audience consciousness if they are sung at events focused upon particular social issues.

[4] An interesting example was Keith Richards' show for the blind, put on by order as a penance after he was found guilty of drug trafficking by a Toronto court (*Maclean's* v.92/19, 1979, p.62).

Another facet of the entanglement of rock and morality has been the use of old hits in advertising. A Toronto journalist suggested boycotting Molson's brewery for using songs by The Beatles in beer advertisements, since she felt things she associated with the songs when they were hits had now been hijacked and appropriated (*Maclean's* v.100/9, 1987, p.32-33). The fact that the advertisement may be the *first* context in which younger people hear the song was one hole in the argument. Nevertheless her approach aligned consumers against the bands and sponsors in a dispute over the ownership of popular memory.

[5] PROCAN was the Performing Rights Organization of Canada. It was set up in 1940 by a similar organization in America, BMI, to licence BMI's catalogue and remunerate musicians when their songs were played in public. In 1990 PROCAN merged with a similar body to become SOCAN.

[6] *Canadian Heritage* (v.15/3, Fall 1989, p.9-11).

6

Waking Up The Neighbours

I don't think I'd ever walk away from Canada.
- Bryan Adams[1]

As the 1980s gave way to the 1990s super-manager Bruce Allen
was facing a mounting series of financial problems. In 1989 his
bid to buy the BC Lions football team fell through when a
recalculation of their debts showed that the team owed
$2.6million. The next year the ventures he had developed with
Lou Blair got into difficulty: not only was Loverboy a spent
force, but the Vancouver nightclub kingdom owned by Allen and
Blair also began to suffer. First, someone who broke an arm
while being ejected from the Club Soda filed a $65,000 lawsuit.
Then a suit ten times as large arose from a similar incident at
their 86th Street club. The Club Soda was renamed The Big Easy

and run by new management directly responsible to a committee containing Allen and Blair (along with Sam Feldman and Roger Gibson), but 86th Street had to be taken over by the receiver.

Despite these setbacks, Allen was still at the centre of a sprawling net of enterprises. On one hand he represented the talented producers Bob Rock and Bruce Fairbairn, and also managed some new acts through Bruce Allen Talent Promotions, such as the Seattle grunge rockers Hall Of Fame. On the other, Sam Feldman's booking agency, Feldman & Associates, was now bringing in $1million per month by matching up Canadian promoters with touring bands. The veteran partners also owned A&F Holdings and two publishers: A&F Music and SLF&A Music Services (for film and TV scoring). Furthermore, Allen had backed the Chip & Pepper wet wear clothing line, put money behind NASCAR indie car racing and even overseen boxing matches.

By 1991 Allen was having to fend off more press speculation than usual. His new boy Paul Laine and the Penta label had sunk into obscurity. Meanwhile, Bob Rock was too busy producing other metal acts to get around to recording his own long-awaited album project. Allen co-produced a Canadian concert week called Music '91 that was funded as a tourism initiative and he cleverly arranged for the Junos to come to Vancouver in the midst of it all. Yet he could not get his top act - Bryan Adams - to play the awards because Adams was touring Europe with ZZ Top. Bryan, in turn, had still not finished his new material. Annoyed by the veil of secrecy that Allen and his charge maintained, the Canadian press started to reconsider their allegiances to Adams. In his absence, they began to celebrate other acts.

For Bryan Adams to be touring so extensively just then was a sign in itself, since he had avoided any big tours for about three years. Such a significant time out of the spotlight was an unusually long interval for Bryan. It indicated all was not well in the Adams camp. The relative failure of *Into The Fire* was bound to take its toll, and Jim Vallance perhaps bore the brunt of it. By mid-1987 the Adams / Vallance pair had written around 100 songs together and they scheduled more sessions for early the next year. However, sometime after they had started writing for the next album, the two began to drift apart.

It would have been easy for Adams to question Vallance and use him as a scapegoat for all that went wrong with the previous album: its sound was too high tech, with too many keyboards and not enough guitar mayhem. For his part, Vallance claimed that he eventually left Bryan because he could no longer stand being at the receiving end of the rocker's childish fits. Whoever made the prime move, although the two men remained on reasonable terms, their rift ended an era of close co-operation. While some partnerships break up under the pressure of fame, it seemed the stigma of failure proved to be too much for Vancouver' s premier song writing duo, especially since Vallance had spent the previous year writing for bands on his own terms.

Alone, Adams was restless. Certainly he had the ability to write good – if not brilliant – material by himself: 'Straight From The Heart' had been a solo composition that gained American chart placing. However, Bryan produced his best work as part of a team, and he began to look for other people who could complete the job that he and Vallance had started.

When an attempt to record with his old friend Bob Clearmountain proved unsatisfactory, Adams began to scout for a partner on the other side of the Atlantic. He approached an Englishman who had produced some of the biggest names in British pop, Steve Lillywhite, but their collaboration came to nothing. Then, after all the misspent hours, Bryan finally settled

down to work with Mutt Lange, the big, blonde, iron-fisted hard
rock producer who had coaxed many a classic from bands such
as AC/DC and Foreigner. Although a few of the songs that
Adams had first draughted with Vallance were retained, in his
darkest hour Bryan scrapped at least an album's worth of
material that consisted of perhaps a year and a half's worth of
work. Once he had a suitable new environment and new partner,
things could begin to happen again.

Mutt was known for a very specific approach to song writing,
which can be heard, for example, echoing through Def Leppard's
Hysteria LP. His method was to base songs around vocal chants.
Mutt's technique didn't clash with Bryan's way of thinking, since
both men were vocalists. In fact, they became good friends.
Adams even took up Lange's vegan diet and began to explore his
Eastern religious outlook.

Together the pair reworked old ideas and picked over fresh ones.
They suffered from no shortage of material. By 1990 the
popularity of groups like the Travelling Willberries and Black
Crowes showed that party rock still had a substantial audience.
Mutt used his preconception of Bryan's image – the idea of the
naughty rocker who had fun (strangely forgetting all the politics
since *Reckless*) - to address Adams' musical needs. The two men's
shared appreciation of the way that Paul Roger's vocals in Bad
Company sometimes sounded like Bryan's also had an influence
on proceedings. Soon enough, Adams and Lange forged 12 out
of the 15 tracks which were to eventually appear on the next
album. It was then that Michael Kamen approached the pair to
complete his song for the film, Robin Hood: Prince of Thieves.

'Everything I Do (I Do It For You)' was a huge success, but as a
result it became a central focus of disputes while Adams was on
the road. Kamen was concerned that he had not been credited
enough in his own creation; so Adams and his manager literally

sent him a donkey as a graphic hint about what sort of song he
had originally sent them. Morgan Creek, a music outfit affiliated
with the movie studio that made Robin Hood, also rush released
a soundtrack compilation album containing Adams' single,
before his own album was ready. The whole episode confirmed
that Bryan's alliance with Hollywood was rather unstable. He had
little time for their pretentious trappings or double dealings and
it was easy to get roped into projects where, as a music man, he
had very little control.

In Britain it was suggested that Adams' new ballad sounded like
'Sailing' by Rod Stewart, and that was hardly surprising as
Bryan's real roots were in fact in British glam rock.[2] Although the
Groover from Vancouver was keen on T-Rex as a youngster, the
'Sailing' claim ignored all the other bands he had been interested
in from Elton John to AC/DC. It was really an attempt to relate
his success to the tastes of a British audience.

Yet another, more important battle erupted in November 1991
when David Duke - an arch-racist who had, a few years earlier,
claimed Canada as one of the last bastions of the white race
while he toured there - took to using Bryan's hit ballad as he
contested the Louisiana State elections.

Duke began to use the song as part of his slide show, the idea
being to demonstrate that he was 'doing it for' his daughters and
by extension the children of all voters. When Adams heard that
his song had been appropriated for use in Duke's governorship
campaign, a battery of lawyers was sent out to consider the
legalities of the issue. Since David Duke was not actually
broadcasting the song, he could not be stopped under copyright
laws, but instead Adams contacted the newspapers to deny any
connections with the politician and implored Louisiana radio
stations not to play his song until after the State elections were

over. It was an admirable move, losing him potential royalties
from that area.

In his home country Adams' single was the forerunner of an
album which he would use as a key weapon in rallying public
support over his struggle about the role and methods of the
national media. Canadian radio regulations gave Bryan a bee in
his bonnet and when his new LP was released, he decided to
speak out about the issue. In order to explain Adams' pivotal role
in that debate it is important to examine Canadian broadcasting
rules in more detail.

Unlike the USA, the Canadian constitution contains no clause
upholding freedom of the press. By claiming to act in the interest
of a public who were, perhaps ironically, otherwise consuming
foreign music, the government could therefore intervene in
broadcasting.[3] Based upon the expedient - if unrealistic - notion
of a unified Canadian media, the Canadian Radio-Television and
Telecommunications Commission (CRTC) was mandated by a
1968 Broadcasting Act to promote national culture. The
Commission's hold over radio licences allowed it to use a gamut
of stipulations that regulated the entire programming
environment in which broadcasters could operate.

The CRTC therefore had the power to impose rules upon
Canadian broadcasters on behalf of the country's embryonic
recording industry, in effect to give Canadian bands a leg-up into
the national spotlight. After nearly a year of preparation, on the
18th of January 1971, special new Canadian content ('Cancon')
regulations were introduced for that purpose. At first they were
for AM stations, but similar regulations soon followed for those
on the FM dial.

The Cancon ruling aimed to introduce Canadian music to
Canadians and therefore to stimulate the country's sound

recording industry. It required that 30% of songs broadcast in
every 4 hour period would qualify as Canadian content.[4] The way
to define what qualified as Canadian became known as the
MAPL system. Each selection (individual song played on the
radio) would be judged against the four following criteria:

M) Music composed by a Canadian.
A) Artist principally performing the music or lyrics must
be Canadian.
P) Performance recorded in, or broadcast live from,
Canada.
L) Lyrics written by a Canadian.[5]

If a song met at least two of the four criteria it qualified as
Canadian content under the regulation. With their system, the
CRTC carefully defined the ownership and nationality of each
song in order to pave the way for optimal social and industrial
consequences.

Since the CRTC aimed to help the entire national music industry,
not just Canadian *artists*, material written by Canadians but sung
by foreigners *could* qualify: under MAPL the Commission's
definition of Canadian talent went beyond the artist who sang
the song, to consider the writer and place of recording.[6]
However, all that the public saw or heard was the artist in the
spotlight, not the songwriter. Since it was possible for a foreign
song sung by a Canadian to fail to meet the other criteria, the
MAPL system always faced problems of public accountability.

Doubts about the aims and diplomacy of Cancon had always
existed in some quarters. Unease about the value of promoting
Canadian talent grew when it was revealed that, while the quota
increased airplay devoted to Canadian music four fold (from 8%
to 30%), sales figures for Canadian acts remained constant at

around 11% - a mere fraction of all the popular music bought within the country.

The sad statistics ignored the fact that most Cancon was provided by independent labels, so there was a vast imbalance in the money spent to promote Canadian releases and the budgets spent to push foreign artists.[7] It was actually some of Canada's biggest artists who, as popular public figures, proved particularly troublesome for the Commission, because those artists straddled the boundary between the public and recording industry. They could question to whom the CRTC was accountable. Some didn't like the way that their radio plays had come about. The new environment raised doubts about their talent that sales figures alone could not always dispel.[8] Such doubts laboured under the unlikely proviso that station programmers were impartial judges of talent in the first place.

While many artists were thankful for the benefits that the Cancon quota could offer them, Bryan Adams had complained about Cancon for some time. Traditionally, because the industry itself had put on a united front in favour of maintaining the MAPL system and the CRTC received so little public complaint on the matter, they rarely revisited the structure of the policy.[9] However, controversy became imminent in the 1990s because Bryan Adams was known to be collaborating with a foreigner; it seemed unlikely that the material on his new album would qualify.

Adams had attained a level of success that was difficult for the Commission to ignore. Though not always a favourite with the critics, Bryan had, by his past success, set a series of precedents for Canadian artists. With the album *Reckless* he had been the first Canadian act to sell over a million copies at home. By September 1991 he was arguably the best known Canadian citizen outside the country. Adams' success abroad had made him a national hero back home with the public, as well as a rallying point for the Canadian recording industry.[10] Moreover, he was fresh from having '(Everything I Do) I Do It For You' : the most successful song ever in Canadian history. A&M were in the distinctly unusual position of releasing an album 15 weeks after its scout single had cleaned up, selling 3 million copies in the USA alone. If that was not enough, the album had shipped an unbelievable 1.2 million copies before even reaching consumers. They knew they had something remarkable on their hands.

Rumours were running wild. Adams' album project was thought to have notched up recording costs of over $1 million, including everything that was not used. On the 23rd of September, years behind schedule, the long-awaited album, *Waking Up The Neighbours*, was finally released. What came to light was that, from the 18 months spent collaborating with Jim Vallance, only four co-written songs were included. Adams and Lange had reinvented those numbers and the ballad from Michael Kamen. The pair also worked with Keith Scott and Vicki Russell (who had now ended her relationship with Bryan) on 'Hey Honey I'm Packing You In,' and contributed another 10 tracks by themselves. That made the album 15 tracks in total. Any other artist would probably have stretched it out as a double LP, but Bryan apparently decided that he wanted to give his fans value for money. It was a way to show them he was firmly returning to the fold as a good-timing rocker, with 'Everything I Do (I Do It For You)' as the exceptional track. Adams had now seemed to realize it made more sense to major on up-beat material and include only one or two ballads per album.

To bring the tracks to life Bryan Adams' road band were on hand, now officially recognized as The Dudes of Leisure, and incidental musicians were also credited with honorary membership of the group. Some songs were laid down in

England, at Battery Studios, but others were recorded at The Warehouse in Canada for a change of scene. Bob Clearmountain went over to the UK to mix the album at Mayfair Studios so, in the event, most of the project was recorded on Mutt's turf. Furthermore, it seemed that things had sprawled on the publishing front: this time the songs were copyrighted to Badams Music and (presumably Bruce Allen's) Zachary Creek Music, as well as to A&M. All of these enterprises would only see profit if the songs could sell, and they could only sell well if they resonated with the audience.

If the excitement surrounding *Waking Up The Neighbours* suggested it would be Adams' best work, the unfortunate reality was that many songs on the album seemed almost too broad for anybody's tastes. Adams himself admitted "I did a party album" so it was inevitable that the new material would be compared to *Reckless,* the pinnacle of his work with Jim Vallance.[11] Mutt's technique was to get the tribal chant of his anthems into the listener with well-placed backing vocals and repetition as key weapons. The new album had clearly borne his musical stamp. The pity was that Adams had previously expressed more of his own style, but now some of the songs bordered on trite. With Vallance, Bryan had crafted songs that were heartfelt, rock in the raw. Even though they were given a severe polishing in the studio, the numbers retained a certain economy. His vocals never hung around in any part of each song long enough to let things get boring.

When a band had either decided to keep vocals high in the mix (as in Loverboy's 'Lovin' Every Minute Of It') or had strong ideas of their own, Mutt's co-operation had worked well in the past. Now Adams was rather at sea. Much of the new material was turgid, ballooning out, despite a reasonable arrangement of the main sounds. At best, in tracks such as 'Can't Stop This Thing We Started,' it all came together. Other songs had occasional highs, like the assertive verse of 'All I Want Is You,' which clearly rocked out. Yet some tracks, including 'Don't Drop That Bomb On Me,' sounded almost like textbook Def Leppard. Even the drums were sampled, a crime better suited to the likes of Alice Cooper! Furthermore Adams blatantly stole from his old songs, the clearest example being the start of 'House Arrest' which more than loosely resembled 'Hearts On Fire' from his last LP.

The only other trace of *Into The Fire* on the new collection was the inclusion of a couple of new tracks where Adams expressed his latest political concerns: 'Vanishing' proved a surprisingly evocative plea to retain treasured buildings, while 'Don't Drop That Bomb On Me' was an over-generalized attack on environmental ills and nuclear dangers. Its message of caring about the world we live in is more than buried by the mood and character of the song. The only thing making it less embarrassing than 'Another Day' was that the number lacked focus. Since Adams never had an ironic character or approach, any ironic reading of such songs is blocked: the only way we can hope they work is as a subliminal attempt to motivate the listener. It seems that Adams had not learned from *Into The Fire* that social causes can become trivialized if they are relegated to unsuitable or second rate compositions. To be fair, however, many stars wouldn't have had the nerve to attempt such material.

In sum, Adams and Mutt delivered a sub-par collection consisting mostly of Lange-style rock tracks, with 'Everything I Do (I Do It For You),' which was aided by outside input, proving the exception. From nearly anyone else it would have been forgivable; knowing what Bryan Adams is capable of, it was frankly disappointing.

The sleeve of *Waking The Neighbours* showed Bryan leaning back to shout through a megaphone, with his Stratocaster strapped on at the ready. He'd donned the recurrent leather jacket and underneath it had regained a white tee shirt. The smart shirted, self-effacing muso had given way once more to a defiant rocker persona, and the album's ear-splitting title was a way to show that his music could be used to cause a stir. "Bryan Adams [is] waking up the neighbours" by playing his music too loud, it implied.

On one hand, Bryan used his new music to revert to a role in public consciousness as the slightly naughty but hard-touring Canadian rocker. On the other, he made use of that image to turn one of his long-standing personal irritations into a full blown public outcry. Since all 15 songs on *Waking Up The Neighbours* had been co-written with Mutt, each song received just one of the two MAPL points needed for it to qualify as Cancon.

Because each song had to be put into the pool of non-qualifying selections, the ones that stations could play 70% of the time, on any FM station in Canada each track could only be played a maximum of 18 times per week. Consequently, Adams knew that he had sacrificed his position in the smaller pool of releases meeting Cancon requirements, but he also had the knowledge that his success could not be attributed to regulation or be used in praise of the Commission. There were actually various mechanisms Adams could have used, even at the last moment, to make the album qualify as Cancon.[12] One possibility was that Bruce Allen may have simply forgotten to file the songs correctly with A&M. Yet since within Canada every label put the MAPL logo on its discs as a marketing device, they would probably not have let such a mistake slip through. Perhaps the mis-filing was a deliberate act by Allen on behalf of his biggest client.

Canadian radio broadcasters kept out of the dispute, but since Adams songs were played on most formats anyway as proven hits, it seems likely they would have preferred that the new

material qualified as Cancon. In fact, neither Adams nor his
manager planned to fight the CRTC decision directly by
contacting the Commission; they knew that Adams would
receive plenty of Canadian airplay as a proven star.[13] Bryan's
unprecedented success and representative status as a regular guy
put him in a particularly powerful position from which to call the
perceived bureaucratic tendencies of the CRTC to account and
criticize Cancon. Bruce Allen and his act were therefore *in a good
position* to question the efficacy of the MAPL system and call the
Commission to account.

First, Allen took the opportunity to challenge Cancon in the
press as a system of allocation of musical privileges.[14] He noted
how other acts - such as The Osmonds with 'Puppy Love'
(written by Canadian Paul Anka) - could qualify when they were
not Canadians, but he didn't examine the industrial aim of
Cancon. Then Allen implicitly compared Cancon to another
allocation system. He pointed out that Canadian sports star
Wayne Gretzky had an American wife, lived in Los Angeles and
paid taxes to the US government, yet he qualified to play on the
Canadian national hockey team. Interestingly Adams' manager
didn't choose to look at other such systems within the music
industry - like the Junos or FACTOR (a government award and
loan scheme for Canadian bands) – or to examine the reasons
why different selection criteria arose in different contexts. To cap
off his effort, Allen then set in train a semantic manipulation that
misleadingly focused the issue on Bryan Adams' own citizenship.

The CRTC implied that Adams' new songs did not qualify as
Canadian content. At the album release party Allen then said
"Try walking up to Bryan and saying 'Hey, guess what Bryan?
You've lived here all your life but you're not a Canadian artist.'"[15]
Adams himself chose the start of his Canadian tour early in 1992
to attack Cancon as part of a series of interviews with Canadian
newspapers. He began by disputing the Commission's relevance:

"If they think my music's un-Canadian that's their problem."
The Canadian rocker then went on to portray himself as their
victim by saying "Who wants to have an international record and
then be declared un-Canadian?"[16] With a sleight of hand usually
practiced by politicians, Allen and his act had turned around
interpretations of the Cancon ruling towards Adams' own
citizenship status as a Canadian, yet nobody had ever said he was
not one. In fact, his citizenship as an artist was the one MAPL
point that he had received!

This perceived miscategorization created a stream of
commentary from the Canadian press which was largely in
favour of Adams and angry at his plight. The Commission was
labelled as self-indulgent and self-perpetuating, even though only
a tiny fraction of its staff dealt with radio Cancon.[17]

Attention was also focused upon why Adams *should* have
qualified: he had a Canadian passport, had already been
recognized by the government (with the Orders of BC and of
Canada), had achieved unprecedented success and did things that
contributed to the nation.[18] Certainly these were all true. From
the way that Bryan had used his nationality against the odds as a
foreign marketing technique to his central efforts in the 'Tears
Are Not Enough' single, he had evidently done good things,
frequently contributed to the cause of national unity, and
exercised an unusual degree of moral control over the use of his
songs.

Furthermore, the notion of Adams as a regular Canadian guy was
drawn upon: he had lived in Canada most of his life, was not a
politician, but was 'very' Canadian.[19] Anne Murray, whose
recordings rarely qualified as MAPL because she sang songs
written by foreigners, also lent her support.[20] However, if an
artist's Canadian citizenship *alone* had been enough for songs that
they sang to qualify as Cancon, the industrial aim of the

regulation would fail. The point was that the public hardly knew or cared about that aim.

Adams himself used the opportunity to put forward his views on the role of the Canadian government.[21] He argued that they did not belong in the music business and that Cancon should have been abolished so that all Canadians could compete on the same footing with the rest of the world. The fact that Canadian consumers only supported him significantly once his music broke in the USA was used to suggest the system was ineffective with them.

In addition Adams claimed Canada's best pop artists [those biggest in the USA] emerged before the regulations had commenced. Bryan argued that labels at home could safely sign Canadian acts in the knowledge that those artists would receive airplay, but because Cancon bred mediocrity Canadian artists could not get signed elsewhere. Since Cancon did not support the bigger Canadian artists who used industry support outside the country, the regulation provided a limited opportunity to support artist career growth.

Adams concluded that mediocrity can never be erased by penalizing excellence, but because audiences cannot be regulated, real talent always wins out. He said if Cancon must stay, then anybody with a Canadian passport should automatically be given two points, but direct support would be better perhaps limited to 2 albums per artist. In other words, in order for Canadian artists to rise from the street they should be rewarded in future solely on the quality of their music.

While some of these comments contained a grain of truth, most were naive or hypocritical.[22] The hypocrisy related to the fact that Adams was flexible in pushing for whatever he could get. As a national hero who was decrying his perceived miscategorization, for many members of the public Bryan had a case. In a Gallup survey held at the time, 76% of those interviewed said Adams was wrongly disqualified and right to make his complaint.[23]

The Commission was in trouble: it knew the industry wanted to keep Cancon and that Adams had lost credibility with smaller musicians, but members of the public were phoning up in droves to complain about the rule.[24] An added problem, to the initiated, was the CRTC's own incoherence.[25]

In British Columbia, former Environment minister John Reynolds wrote to Prime Minister Brian Mulroney complaining that even though Bryan was "a full time ambassador' for Canada, the CRTC had seen fit to disqualify him.[26] Mulroney quietly prompted the Commission Chairman to set up a committee of music industry representatives in order to study the controversy and make policy recommendations. A date was set on paper for a review of submissions, and both newspapers and regional offices were told about the issue. Irate callers were advised to write to the CRTC, because, unlike the initiation of MAPL, the process of this review was on paper, without any public hearings. Effectively the CRTC had been forced to quietly grapple with the most embarrassing but least radical of Adams' complaints.

Before the decision of the CTC was announced, a significant incident took place some 16 months later. The Juno awards, which are nationally televised on CBC and partly State-funded, were held March 26th. As a rather stuffy award system, there was never any room for more than one star of each type. Adams had won numerous Junos in previous years – including 6 of them for the songs on *Reckless* in 1984 - but in doing so he inevitably put other Canadian male vocalists in the shade. In the past, Adams had fended off Corey Hart, but in 1992 the Red Rider veteran Tom Cochrane was nominated against him in 5 categories.

The atmosphere was tense: since the awards represented votes from members of CARAS, they could be used as a forum for the industry to pass public comment on Adams' views. Cochrane had achieved success only within Canada. His latest album *Mad, Mad World* seemed a strong contender for industry support. Adding to the tension was the fact that Bruce Allen had formerly managed the new contender without financial success and was rumoured to have threatened to pull Bryan unless his star was guaranteed an award.[27]

As it turned out, in the categories where both Cochrane and Adams had been nominated, the Red Rider singer won three awards (album, single and male vocalist) and Adams won two (songwriter and producer). Of these, Cochrane's awards were all selected by CARAS votes, while Adam's producer award was chosen by a CARAS panel.

Bryan also got a Special Achievement Award for his bestselling single, and - characteristically reverting to regular guy status - he thanked CARAS for "putting aside the politics."[28] The net result was that the industry had expressed some disagreement with Adams' views; a CARAS survey taken on the night found that only 12% of members thought Cancon was ripe for reconsideration.[29] Also, as a result of Cochrane's new-found recognition, his label gave his album a new impetus in the USA.

Despite disagreeing with Adams' opinions, CARAS had decided to recognize the phenomenal success of 'Everything I Do (I Do It For You)', and they were not alone in doing so. Bryan got shortlisted for 6 Grammys and received 4 of them. He was even nominated for an Oscar.

Preferring constant publicity to the idea of bowing out on a high note, A&M released several singles from Adams' new album throughout 1992, all of which got reasonable chart placings. The success of the new material allowed Bryan to re-establish his place in the popular consciousness. Lazy TV programmers in Hong Kong even used his video to fill in time between programmes for several weeks.

Meanwhile Bryan decided to keep his touring machine (which now included a mobile swimming pool) on the road. In January 1992, to a jubilant crowd which included his (now remarried) mother, the Groover from Vancouver played the Pacific Coliseum in his hometown. Adams mentioned to the crowd that although he came from West Vancouver (a middle class area), he at one stage lived down in the (working class) suburb of Surrey. The declaration raised squeals of delight because it confirmed precisely what fans wanted to believe: that Bryan Adams really was an ordinary working class kid made good. Like a whirlwind, in early February the Adams entourage continued over to Australia. Their long sets featured material almost exclusively from *Reckless*, the new album, and *Cuts Like A Knife*: it seemed that Adams was back in party mode.

By the middle of the year Adams went to Europe and, although he missed the Canada Day celebrations at home, as one of a handful of UK dates he entertained some 65,000 fans at Wembley Stadium. Later in July, Bryan did a set in Istanbul, making him the first Western star to rock Moslem fans from that area.

As the year progressed he arrived back in Canada to make the largest tour across the country that was ever attempted by a Canadian artist. Adams played in front of 146,000 fans across 13 cities. By tapping previously unserved secondary markets in smaller areas, he eventually grossed $9 million; an impressive figure for any Canadian tour.

Finally, late in January 1993 the CRTC announced its decision on how songs resulting from international collaborations might be interpreted under the MAPL system. Ever since the commission's chairman called upon music industry representatives to examine the issue, the general view was that Cancon was a good rule, but it would need some fine tuning to avoid more cases like that of Bryan Adams.[30] In so far that it was cheap, effective and easy to use, Cancon had all the advantages of a blunt instrument. The option of awarding half points would make the assessment of songs and other administration difficult.

The CRTC eventually decided to award one whole point if it could be shown that a Canadian co-writer contributed at least 50% to both the music and lyrics of any composition. Since the ruling only applied to albums made after September 1991, *Waking Up The Neighbours* had effectively been the stimulus to change but did not qualify.[31]

The ruling meant that the CRTC had to face a new problem: frequently, nobody could be sure exactly how much each person contributed to any co-written song. Perhaps more importantly the new rule showed that significant changes were occurring. First, while Cancon quotas could previously be addressed on a station-by-station basis, the new rule represented an unprecedented historic alteration in the MAPL system itself.[32] Second, it effectively enlarged the pool from which programmers could draw qualifying material, making more contributions to Cancon possible from the majors. Sony Music, for example, had a policy of encouraging international co-writes.

Into the 1990s Adams therefore managed to accelerate out of a musical rough patch, not only by finding a new environment and partner - and recording a runaway ballad - but returning to a stereotype in which he was already recognized: the regular rocker. His politics had come full circle, however. While Bryan had previously been naive in lending his weight to others' concerns he now craftily stage-managed his involvement and used the full force of his image to portray himself as victim.

As a forum for expressing talent, Cancon inevitably had mixed results. Like any policy it could not please all the people all of the time. Stimulated by Adams' efforts, the CRTC, as a nationally accountable organization, had to consider something beyond its scope: the international mingling of staff that characterized the upper echelons of the sound recording industry. Unfortunately Adams' protests tended to draw attention away from the more local end of the industry: the rookie Canadian bands on the circuit that, if they had potential, were given a break by Cancon.

These smaller bands now had to compete with Bryan Adams once more. Whatever anyone really thought of the issue, it was, to date, probably Bryan's most successful - and most ominous - political manoeuvre.

---

[1] *Saturday Night* (v.107/9, 1992, p.82).

[2] 'Rock of Ages Still Endures' by R. Sandall (*Sunday Times* 4/9/92, Section 6,
p.8).

[3] See Hindley et al (1977, p.90). In the USA the Federal Communications Commission (FCC) deals with radio station licensing. Since the First Amendment guarantees freedom of the press the FCC cannot censor stations *a priori*.

It can, nonetheless, remove a licence if the station broadcasts content that is not in the public interest. Coupled with vague directives, the threat of such action has induced stations to police themselves and avoid drug-related lyrics (Denisoff, 1986, p.272).

4 *Canadian Composer* (no.200, 1985, p.22).

5 Basic MAPL information is taken here from TC Factsheet: The MAPL System (CRTC, RI-02-92). The CRTC liberally define a "Canadian" person as a Canadian citizen, landed immigrant or person living in Canada for at least the last six months.

6 The 'P' criterion makes the location where a song was recorded an important consideration. It is one example of the international nature of the recording industry denied by Cancon: bands have often left Canada to record with producers they like (*Nite Moves* 10/92, p.13) or to avoid the pressure, disturbances or boredom of recording at home (*Canadian Musician* v.1/5, 1989, p.92).

Conversely, bands who came to Canada, for example to work with producer Bruce Fairbairn in Vancouver, received their 'P' point in the system. This configuration of MAPL has created revenue and put Canada on the map for fans abroad. However, whether its benefits relate to the overall aims of Cancon remains questionable.

7 *The Record* (v.12/4, 1991, p.22).

8 In formats with less Canadian material, Canadian acts were getting played because of their nationality rather than how good they were. If things like promotional dollars were held equal, low sales could show that a band was given an artificial break by Cancon, but sceptics could also dismiss high sales as a result of guaranteed exposure (Wright, 1987, p.30). As competition to fill quotas became tougher, the reasoning behind this judgement began to fall down.

[9] For example, the Canadian Songwriters Association found threats to Cancon a key worry for their members (*Probe* v.2/6, 1987, p.2) and performing rights society magazines contained editorials mobilizing Canadian writers against any erosion of the rule (cg. *Music Scene* no.345, 1985, p.2).

[10] The team of Adams and Vallance were leading members of a Canadian performing rights society called PROCAN. Editorials in their magazine *Canadian Composer* co-opted Adams, while Vallance joined PROCAN's staff (*Music Scene* v.3/5, 1987, p.2; *Probe* v.2/4, 1987, p.1). In 1991, after PROCAN was reformulated as SOCAN, personal differences with its president - possibly connected with the star's international view of song writing - meant that Adams defected to ASCAP, the American performing rights organization.

[11] *Saturday Night* (v.107/9, 11/92, p.80).

[12] For instance, since some of the initial single's lyrics were taken from the Robin Hood film script and Michael Kamen wrote the melody they could have fudged the credits so that Adams appeared to write either the music or lyrics, giving the song 2 MAPL points. Furthermore, Mutt and Adams had reworked Adams' ideas for many of the songs (*Vancouver Sun* 27/1/92 p.C4), so this fudging could have been done on other songs. Also, as some of the album was recorded in Canada, in theory some songs could have been given the 'P' point.

[13] *Winnipeg Free Press* (13/9/91, p.31).

[14] *Globe and Mail* (13/9/91, p.C1).

[15] *Calgary Herald* (13/9/91, p.F2).

[16] *Montreal Gazette* (14/1/92, p.C27); *Toronto Star* (14/1/92, p.B1).

[17] The CRTC has around 375 staff and 9 of them deal with Cancon on radio (*Financial Times of Canada* 18/2/91, p.10). Thus because stations largely police themselves only 3% of staff need to administer Cancon.

[18] *Winnipeg Free Press* (13/9/91, p.39).

[19] See *Performing Arts* (v.27/2, 1992, p.16). "Although he claims to feel 'very Canadian', Adams says that he has never thought of his music as having a national sound" (N. Jennings, *Maclean's* v.100/27, 1987, p.35).

[20] *Vancouver Sun* (16/1/92, p.D6).

[21] His argument here is drawn from interviews in *The Toronto Star* (14/1/92, p.B1) and *Vancouver Sun* (27/1/92, p.C1+C4).

[22] Adams was naive, for instance, because he ignored how programmers formed and picked from pools in their different formats. He was hypocritical in querying the whole system but focusing attention upon getting one rule changed. He stressed quality while using the charts as an arbiter. He claimed to be apolitical whilst beginning a change many politicians would not

have had the power to make. Furthermore Adams was far from being against any State involvement in cultural industries, in that he supported the CBC as "a form of government subsidized entertainment that actually does some good." (*Saturday Sight* v.107/9, 1992, p.84).

23 *Halifax Chronicle Herald* (5/3/92, p.B1).

24 *Vancouver Sun* (16/1/92, p.16).

[25] As acting director for radio at the CRTC, Anne Marie Desroches told the press that Adams' album had missed by half a point, due to its foreign co-writer. Yet the CRTC never gives out half points (*Winnipeg Free Press* 13/9/91, p.39).

Furthermore, CRTC factsheets (like RI-02-92) used the confusing shorthand of selections qualifying as "Canadian" rather than meeting Cancon requirements.

[26] *BC Report* (v.3/5, 30/9/91, p.39).

[27] Canadian Business (v.57/9, 1984, p.74); Globe and Mail (30/3/92, p.A2).

28 Backstage he added "If politics are going to be involved then let it be the way it's going to be," while Cochrane said at one point "Anyone who thinks Canadian music is mediocre can go to hell." (*Globe and Mail* 30/3/92, pp.A2, A1).

29 *CARAS News* (2/92, p.2).

[30] *Vancouver Sun* (16/1/92, p.D6).

[31] *Vancouver Sun* (1/2/93, p.D8).

[32] Until the co-write rule the way the MAPL system applied to each song was immutable. For example, although in its first year songs with 1 MAPL qualified, the CRCT made it clear that changes to a writer's citizenship would not alter the MAPL rating of their previous songs (*Canadian Composer* no.57, 1971, p.32).

7

Conclusion

**It's tough having heroes. It's the hardest
thing in the world. It's harder than being a
hero... hero-worshippers (fans) must live with
the continually confirmed dread of hero
slippage.**

- Lester Bangs[1]

In the previous chapters, Bryan Adams demonstrated through
his activities that he is probably one of the most irregular of
regular guys in popular music. On one hand he has become
known as a man still dedicated to his music and life on the road.
He remains an excellent songwriter, a fluent guitarist, and a
talented singer who lives for his performances. On the other
hand, Adams has also emerged as a champion of diverse causes
and someone quick to complain against what he sees as the
world's ills.

Chapter 7

Since history is always something in the making, it is important to address the question of what Bryan Adams and his close supporting cast are likely to do from now on, before the story of the Canadian star can be fully assessed.

Since he parted company with Bryan, Jim Vallance wrote for a range of bands which have included the likes of Aerosmith, The Scorpions and Alice Cooper. Jim also joined the board of Canada's central performing rights society and in the late 1980s he started actively campaigning for better royalties for songwriters. To stay in the niche that he found, in 1992 Vallance opened Armoury Studios in the beautifully quaint Kitsilano area of Vancouver, not far from downtown. While Adams spent more time in the UK, Vallance preferred to avoid the strain of shuttling between places by firmly pursuing his vocation from home.

Bruce Allen also continued to work, even though by now probably his entire staff could comfortably retire on the money. In the 1990s his goal of re-orientating Bryan Adams to tap the baby boomer market at last came to pass and he continued to work with a range of artists. By late 1992 he had added the Cajun accordion player Zachary Richards to his roster; a sign that, despite his straight down the line demeanour, Allen was becoming more altruistic and experimental in his policies. Then again, perhaps he just loved the challenge. He spent much of the decade hosting Sound Off, a national, issue-orientated Sunday night radio show. Never without an opinion, Allen enthusiastically ruminated on a variety of topics. Another challenge for him was to develop his business interests in sports promotion.

Average rock stars have careers like those of athletes - bursting out like supernovas before bowing out like damn squibs. Despite his ups and downs, Bryan Adams has proven his longevity in the spotlight, itself a testament to his unusual talent and drive. He became a millionaire many times over and could have retired completely in the 1990s to devote full attention towards a budding new interest in off-road racing. Bryan proved himself, however, to be a performer first and foremost, driven by the adrenalin rush of being on stage. At that point retiring was not in his game plan. The traditional older rocker's career move, to be sat full time behind a production console in a recording studio helping newer talent record hits of their own, did not seem to be on the cards. Although Adams had traditionally co-produced his own material, he said in one interview, "I don't touch that job anymore."[2]

To continue with his singing and recording vocation, Bryan planned his own Vancouver recording facility and aimed towards another studio album for 1995. But in the meantime A&M put out a greatest hits package to catch the Christmas 1993 market, with the title of *So Far So Good*. Adams and Lange even composed some new material for it. One song that was released as a single was a ballad called 'Please Forgive Me.' The video showed the earnest rocker wearing a black t-shirt and jeans delivering a tear-jerking rendition in the studio. The band sit about like the crew of a ship which has been too long at sea and the atmosphere is suitably laid back. Even the studio owner's dog is allowed to roam around the gathering. The focus is still on the song, and therefore on its singing. As a consequence the vocals are high in the mix, which seems to be a pattern to which two vocalists like Adams and Lange quite often return (the pair have also written similar new material for Tina Turner). The technique focuses attention back onto the vocalist as the central producer of sounds.

'Please Forgive Me' put Adams back at the helm once again, which suited him fine. In fact, he commissioned remakes for several of his videos based upon spliced-together live footage from various days on the road, to put an emphasis on performance. In a strange way, then, the trappings of fame really didn't change Bryan Adams: he was still reliant on the most obvious way to be a crowd pleaser. After all, as the Vancouver music critic Tom Harrison once said: Adams is no innovator.[3]

With the relatively newfound realization that a well-constructed and unusual ballad could shift millions, Adams stuck to the formula. The Dudes of Leisure accepted his stance as long as they could pump up the action once in a while with a couple of storming hard rock numbers. The question became whether Bryan Adams had enough maturity to become the Frank Sinatra of power ballads and acquire the mantle of a post-military Elvis. Certainly 'Please Forgive Me' helped reinforce his status as one of the most eligible bachelors in rock.

While Adams continued on his path in the early 1990s, it is important to appraise the direction that he came from. Looking back over a buoyant early recording career, it almost seems like Bryan learned from his recorded outings by using the alchemist's model of thesis-antithesis-synthesis: he became famous with an album of strong ballads, lurched over to become a popular rocker, got into social causes, then, a little burned by the most recent experience, drew all of those threads together into a mixed album.

Impure mixtures are never as precious as pure gold, and, speaking personally, *Reckless* remained dominant in my record collection, ranking up there with *Back In Black* by AC/DC. Maybe the songs were textbook and radio-friendly with production tones slick enough to put off the staunch purists. But a lot of musicians would have given their front teeth to have made so startling a classic rock album. The dynamo behind the urgent collection was an extraordinary ambition that perhaps only those on the brink of the big time can fully comprehend, an ambition that made the record burn.

The interesting thing about *Reckless*, and the album before it, was that they were made under such intense pressure from Adams' label. The fact that his other efforts were either less disciplined or less successful seems to indicate that rock primarily exists to seize the moment and thrives on urgency. If such an idea is correct, then - especially if you think that rock should be the appendage of a utopian political project rather than simply an emotional rollercoaster - it's unfortunate side effect is that maybe, by having nothing significant to say, such an album could reflect its moment. Of course, rock can be both emotional and political; it's not a question of either/or.

In the mid-1980s the magic world of popular music was infused with a certain kind of politics. Most bands created apolitical songs that did not address interest-group issues too squarely and then put them in contexts like benefit gigs and charity compilation albums. It made sense, and it worked. It wasn't as if each act had a central motivating political project or claimed to represent a particular social group. Although musicians' popularity lay in other realms, they were asked to participate, co-opted by external causes. The only way an observer could excavate a band's politics was to see which of these causes it supported. Significantly, after being goaded by the critics, Bryan Adams went much further than that, yet his efforts didn't seem to work out. When it arrived, 18 months after *Reckless*, even Bryan himself admitted that *Into The Fire* had been "a bit of a curve ball."[4]

Looking at the facts, Adams made an unusual effort to demonstrate his political concerns. They took over most of the lyrics of an entire album. The move would have been unusual for a mainstream artist even in the 1960s, but in the 1980s it was a freak occurrence. Especially since he was known as such a sensitive, regular guy. The question is precisely where all that effort went wrong, and why it drove away fans?

Perhaps Bryan felt implored to take the diagnosis of the rock press as a prescription to become, as it were, his own Boss. At any rate, at least Springsteen did not become famous for one thing and then do something that was so far away from where he started. The discrepancy was evidence for the argument Adams was merely an opportunist, which is probably why he went so far to prove his commitment. Listening to the album itself, it seems the first reason for Adams' difficulty was probably that he took on the concerns of other people so it was difficult to convincingly play their role in cases where he was not the victim. It was actually a testament to Bryan Adams' middle class roots and self-consciousness that he made the album that way. Regular guys probably would not have had enough integrity to care about the issues raised: it was unlikely that fans found the struggles that Adams selected were relevant to their lives.

Second, what also made the album less authentic was that Adams took on so many concerns. Perhaps more like he was appeasing his own sense of social conscience by making such drastic a swing towards political writing. Fans didn't know much about Bryan Adams, but they knew he hadn't become famous as a champion of ethnic minorities and old soldiers. If listeners could use Bryan's non-image to imagine what kind of a guy he was before, his image could also be used to suggest that his politics belonged to everyone. Diplomatically, with *Into The Fire*, Adams had produced a polished selection box of songs as a tonic for those afflicted with the woes of his era. The album's slick approach in part detracted from its subject matter. The styles of some songs buried those currents of feeling that should have asked us to care about the issues they raised. In short, even if a record could spell out a better future with the highest intentions, if it sounded unconvincing it will fail to inspire.

In an age when popular music was supposed to be about having a good time, playing socially-conscious rock was, perhaps, rather like reading an obituary in the middle of a comic show. Stars could get up on stage and tell everyone to hush up while they delivered a sober monologue, but they were leading people to expect one thing and then suddenly giving them another. Worst still, they sometimes appealed to people's sense of respect as an excuse to do so. However if a performer ignored their duty, or just delivered a few jokes, they were showing no respect and the audience could sense it.

The real answer was to bite the bullet and use all available resources to appropriately convey the gravity of important situations. It could be done, but the main thing was to approach with caution, feeling and sensitivity. To take a specific example, The Beatles had been Bryan Adams' heroes, but it was only after making quite a few albums that they really explored alternative avenues in culture and politics.

Bryan's case may not only have been a matter of too much too fast. For instance, John Lennon eventually wrote some uncannily profound political material, but it was not just because he was a talented musician. Lennon bought his talents fully to bear on the focus of his attention and was not afraid to expose all sides of his personality to the public. Because you knew John's sense of humour, of irony, of struggle, of self, you knew that his protest - his pacifism, his sense of class struggle — was real. He was using his own position to appeal to audiences, rather than exploiting the plight of others. Perhaps Lennon's later life was an indication he had gone too far as he was trying to regain a private sense of self and refrain from the dangers of being set up as a leader.

Chapter 7

Into The Fire was a worthy experiment, but it was one that did not really come together. If it had, a lot of fans - perhaps even the mass marketplace - would probably have backed Adams by buying the album. Perhaps the best thing to come out of the whole episode was that, to demonstrate his commitment, Bryan helped a lot of people and animals with his activities in the late 1980s. As time went by, it became clear that even if his music was not always outstanding and his complaints sometimes a little myopic, he stood by causes in a way that was admirable. In the 1990s he retained his political affiliations, even though he largely dropped the approach to lyrics which had cost him customers who might have bought *Into The Fire*.

Bryan Adams has helped organizations big and small over the years, from the Vancouver Soccer Association and Western Canadian Wilderness Committee to the Prince's Trust and Amnesty International. Furthermore, Adams incurred losses by doing particular things when he wanted to help. For example, when not enough tickets were sold in advance, he put on a free show for fans in Calgary in 1990 and the gesture cost him $200,000. Also he usually remained firm in his stance, refusing, for example, to remove the Greenpeace dedication from his tour programme during dates in Iceland and Japan in 1991.

The Cancon debate was the most graphic example of Bryan Adams retaining his political activity into the 1990s, and it was probably his most successful political venture.

If his interest in building conservation showed that Adams could stage-manage his own complaint, the way he refloated the Cancon issue showed what he could do in a full scale campaign. His relative success resulted from a portrayal of himself as the victim; the misunderstood regular guy who had retained the trappings of a street musician. It was certainly a more effective strategy than his previous efforts, which either avoided specifics or involved him speaking on behalf of others. Those affected most by the new MAPL policy - upcoming bands forced into competition with the big boys on Canadian radio - could not express their interests from the same privileged platform as their famous counterpart. No longer could anybody who looked at all the details label Bryan Adams as simply a naïve and misguided nice guy; he had become a prime mover in the situation.

In the absence of other Canadian stars with international stature, Adams was a figure given a special position by the general public in his home country. In August 1992, the pop chanteuse from Quebec called Celine Dion, by then an international star in her own right, said that both she and Adams were so appalled by the idea of separation within Canada that they were considering recording a duet in praise of national unity. Bryan would once again have been using his citizenship and heroic status within his home country for a particular national-political end. Eventually they did do a live duet together, a version of 'Everything I Do (I Do It For You)' called 'Look Into My Eyes (Everything I Do).'

Perhaps Adams' ability to capitalize on his own image is only part of the picture when compared to the interest other people have shown in hijacking his success. David Duke's campaign showed Bryan was willing to set limits on how far any appropriation of his appeal could go.

On the idea of sponsorship, though, Adams seemed to make a quiet turnaround. Despite Loverboy's 1982 Nissan tour deal, manager Bruce Allen had been sceptical of making mutual deals with corporations wishing to advertise their wares on Adams' tours. Bryan had previously walked out of one meeting with a drinks manufacturer and never endorsed any commodities except for his records. Yet for his Waking Up The Nation tour of Canada in 1992, Adams received the joint backing of Coke and a top national brewery - Molsons. It was an indication of his business acumen, but hardly a wildman thing to do. Perhaps such an attitude demonstrated that Adams took rock onto a new territory where old questions had to be inverted in order to discover the medium's true flexibility? The idea that someone young could play rock so effectively in a conservative (small 'c') way showed that the music was still anybody's ball game. There is something bizarrely reassuring about a guy who, when awarded a Juno, dedicates it to his mother. The gesture showed that rock is still a forum for whatever a person wants to do with it; having to be a rebel is almost as much of a strain as not being allowed to be one.

Perhaps one of the most interesting things about Bryan Adams is that, although compared to those who went before, he was so conservative, he always entered a room with a slight whiff of the rebel about him. If a regular rebel was what was traditionally expected, the question became how much Adams manufactured that edge and how much he lived it.

Questions about the image of Bryan Adams came to a head when, to cap his Waking Up The Nation tour, suggestions were raised that he might do a free gig for his hometown in the communal space of Stanley Park. From the beginning, the idea was controversial. It would have been difficult for Adams to claim he was an environmentalist if his fans trampled the park, left litter, increased downtown traffic congestion and enjoyed noise levels fit to awaken the neighbours.[5] Part of the debate hinged on what his fans were really like. Most people who had taken any notice knew that – especially in Vancouver - they were anybody's kids, not the sort to trash their own backyard. Even the Parks Board gave a limited nod of agreement, if the event could be limited to 42,000 tickets and they could take a share of the merchandising profits.

As local hype reached fever pitch, as if to indicate that there were still some fundamental problems, Bruce Allen suddenly wound down the publicity. An unusually indifferent Adams did the last gig on his Canadian tour some 30 miles away in the tiny town of Osoyoos set in the southern part of BC's Okanagan valley. Adams seemed content enough to let hometown fans take a hike to see the show, buy the $28 t-shirts, and then go home quietly. He carried on regardless, doing a few more US TV slots and a studio set for syndicated radio. Perhaps the entire Stanley Park gig had just been a false alarm manufactured to fuel pride and increase publicity in order to focus attention on the new album?

Fans knew that maybe they'd have to wait a long time for Adams to produce material of the calibre of *Reckless* again, and speaking realistically, life went on in spite of that. Bryan's long and lurching career has shown that to be famous it's always more difficult than might be expected because unexpected pressures arise. When they do, famous people are like any others in negotiating changing contexts however they can. It's more than a coincidence that Bryan Adams rose through the ranks of pop as a "just your meat-and-potatoes, nut-and-bolts type of guy" but ended up, ironically, a vegan.[6]

Adams' music and activities have shown that Bryan is a man of contradictions. Some of those, such as one of his quotes in 1992 - "I never got into this to be a star. The idea of being famous wasn't part of the plan" - are difficult to swallow.[7] They represent a form of image management which ignores the historic facts.

Other contradictions can be forgiven, as they simply reveal that the person behind the image remains mortal: he's not a creation of some marketing expert. Bryan Adams became famous for one thing, and then began to use his fame for something else; that alone was not particularly unusual in the 1980s. What was unusual

Chapter 7

was the way that he was consistent enough to let the two things mix together. It may have been a case of too much too soon - even athletes only became politicians once they retire.

Adams' career is crucially important for anybody interested in the drama by which stars relate to a wider world. The reason is that when heroes with whom we identify step into the spotlight, we begin to question ourselves if they start doing things that we wouldn't. The ultimate paradox is that while Bryan Adams did not necessarily set himself up as anything other than a singer he was, because of his regular image perceived - almost inevitably - as something more.

With rock music, everyone is lucky enough to be left with some escape routes from the problem of unruly heroes. Consumers can celebrate songs rather than singers, and musicians can seize the challenge to do something more consistent with their own sense of integrity. Neither of those options is easy. It's hard to detach yourself and hold back from wanting to get more fascinated with the maker of something as personal and emotional as a song.

From outside the music industry and beyond the glare of public scrutiny, we don't know the full extent of those shifting pressures that might affect anyone who tries to do what their heroes have attempted. But both options bring us closer to what Adams himself always stressed: the central importance of music. When he was asked once how he cracked America, the answer was simple: "Songs, man, songs."[8]

---

[1] Taken from Bangs' book Psychotic *Reactions and Carburettor Dung* (1988, p.161).

[2] Rock World (v. 2/10, 1993, p. 15).

[3] *Saturday Night* (v.107/9, 11/92, p.84).

[4] *Rolling Stone* (No.508, 10/9/87, pp.42-45).

[5] In England, a rather defiant Adams promoted a t-shirt telling the neighbours where to go - with an expletive - if they didn't like it; then bureaucrats came out to measure the decibels produced by his shows (*Canadian Musician* v.14/5, 10/92, p.40).

[6] O'Hara (1992, p.14); *Saturday Night* (v.107/9, 11/92, p.80).

[7] *Saturday Night* (v.107/9, 11/92, p.56).

[8] Robertson (1992, p.11).

Bibliography

Contemporary Sources

The following newspapers, magazines, journals and fact sheets have been referenced within the text:

From Canada:

British Columbia Report

Calgary Herald

Canadian Business

Canadian Composer

Bibliography

Canadian Musician

CARAS News

Chatelaine

CRTC 'The MAPL System' Fact Sheet R1-02-92

The Financial Post

Financial Times of Canada

The Globe and Mail

Halifax Chronicle Herald

Maclean's Magazine

Montreal Gazette

Music Express

Music Scene

Nite Moves

Performing Arts

Probe (supplement Can. Composer)

The Record

Saturday Night

Toronto Star

Vancouver Sun

Winnipeg Free Press

From America:

Billboard

Creem

Guitar Player

Newsweek

The New York Times

Rolling Stone

Spin

Variety

Village Voice

From Britain:

Life & Times (supplement to *The Times*)

Melody Maker

Music Week

Rock World

The Sunday Times

The Times

Bibliography

Bangs, L. 1988. *Psychotic Reactions and Carburetor Dung*. New York: Vintage Books.

Denisoff, S. 1986. *Tarnished Gold: The Record Industry Revisited*. New Brunswick: Transaction Books.

Guterman, J. and O'Donnell, O. 1991. *Slipped Discs*. London: Virgin.

Hindley, M. *et al* 1977. *The Tangled Net: Basic Issues in Canadian Communication*. Vancouver: J.Douglas.

Kamin, P. 1985. *Bryan Adams*. Wauwatosa, Wisconsin: Robus Books.

Meltzer, R. 1987. *The Aesthetics of Rock.* New York: Da Capo.

Nietzsche, F. 1882. *The Gay Science.* London: Penguin.

O'Hara, J. 1989. *Bryan Adams.* Markham, Ontario: Fitzhenry and Whiteside.

Robertson, S. 1992. *Bryan Adams: The Illustrated Biography.* London: Omnibus Press.

Wright, R. 1987. "'Dream, Comfort, Memory, Despair": Canadian Popular Musicians and the Dilemma of Nationalism 1968-1972,' *The Journal of Canadian Studies* 22,4, 27-43.

Afterword

This recent song I wrote with Bryan - I was in Canada and Bryan was in England. We weren't even in the same room when we wrote it. We would send ideas back and forth by email. We would send audio files back and forth. Sometimes we would use Skype or i-Chat to convey ideas back and forth.

- Jim Vallance (2010)[1]

A lot has happened since *Bryan Adams: A Fretted Biography* was first published.

For a start, with the full public adoption of the internet the music field has changed out of all recognition. Bryan Adams and Jim Vallance have also long since buried their differences and occasionally written songs together. Interviewed in 2010,

Afterword

Vallance estimated that in a song writing career spanning over three decades, he had worked on about 300 released songs, with Bryan and many other artists. He added: "I have a real level of comfort working with Bryan... Song writing is really a personal thing. You have to have a level of trust and comfort, and I have that with Bryan." Vallance continued: "We've just done it so much. I think he and I have spent something like 20,000 hours together in a small room with just our guitars."

Times change. Adams himself has expanded his career to alternate between the roles of – who would have guessed – photographer, social activist and rock star. My own interest in his image has been more than matched by his visual interest in the images of other people.

It is worth taking a moment in this afterword to explain how *Bryan Adams: A Fretted Biography* came to be written, its impact, and Bryan's continuing career since it was first published early in 1994.

My first real encounter with Bryan Adams, as a fan, was back in July 1991 when he supported ZZ Top at the Milton Keynes Bowl. I'd heard about him years earlier because my school friends all loved *Reckless*, but since school I'd developed more of an ear for rock music and learned to play electric guitar.

Bryan proved to be an urgent and exciting live performer. It was his stage show that connected with me. Soon after that wonderful initiation, my studies took me to Canada where I participated in the Master's program at UBC. Since my thesis focused on the Canadian music industry, I discovered that I had a great opportunity to examine a national hero. When I returned to England two years and one degree later, I drew together my research and started writing.

Because much of my research was based upon information from the Canadian press, the book was designed to give readers outside of Canada new insights into the emergence and tribulations of a local hero.

Upon returning to the UK, I created a manuscript which I began shopping to various up-scale publishers that had catalogues covering the music biography market. The editor-in-chief of one wrote back to explain:

> It is clear to me from reading your work that you know your subject well and have a good grasp of the way in which the music business works and how Bryan Adams pursued his goals within it. Unfortunately we have no plans to publish... The rock stars whose biographies are commercially successful are those who are controversial, badly behaved, politically outspoken, promiscuous, addicted to drugs and / or alcohol, or dead through their own well-publicized carelessness. Rock stars who are polite and well behaved, but politically neutral and sexually uninteresting just don't sell biographies, no matter how worthy they are. The same would apply to Phil Collins, Mark Knopfler, even Sting. Nevertheless, I was impressed by your work and if the situation changes re:Adams, I'll be in touch.

It was quite a rude awakening in the ways of professional rock writing to find out that the only viable musicians were those who rubbed everyone up the wrong way and died in a pile of their own vomit!

Afterword

On the strength of my manuscript alone, meanwhile, I was offered a job at Sony Music. I decided to self-publish the book at the start of 1994. Well before the era of publishing-on-demand and social media, it was pitched as something in-between a fanzine and a proper publication. Physically assembling each batch of new copies was a process of happy amateurism, as I compiled the pages and stapled the thing together in my parents' living room. I also acquired an ISBN number and would regularly fill in back-orders to restock book shops that ran out of copies up and down the country. Over a decade-long period the biography sold many hundreds of copies. I would even take the train down to London and get it placed in shops like (the now defunct) Tower Records and (still going) Foyles book store. It was all a labour of love.

Thanks to my marketing efforts, the International Council for Canadian Studies recognized and listed the volume. I also received an email from a fellow biographer who had managed to secure a contract with a major publisher and release their own book. They told me that it would have saved them most of their research if they had found my volume earlier. Fans seemed interested in the book, too. One Italian club ordered twenty copies at once for their convention. Letters poured in from Bryan Adams fans all over the world, a few of whom had embarrassingly long, pre-internet swap lists of Adams' recorded material. One devotee even promised to get a copy of the book across to Adams' mother. My favourite letter, though, was from a teacher at a British middle school who ordered a copy as a present for his female pupil when she was convalescing from an operation to remove a brain tumour.

Living people have a frustrating habit of outpacing their biographers, especially if they are as active and hard-working as Bryan Adams. In 1994, fresh from a joint ballad with Sting and Rod Stewart, Adams gave British fans a treat when he rocked

Wembley and Gateshead. His label A&M kept the ball rolling by releasing *Live! Live! Live!* - an album that was previously only available as an expensive import. In 1996 I wrote an assessment of Bryan's next studio album, *18 Til I Die*:

> My initial reaction to Adams' new material was a twinge of disappointment: why did it take so long to arrive? Why hadn't they put on those reasonable boogie B-sides ('Lowlife,' 'Hey Elvis,' etc.) or the disputed 'Rock Steady,' or even that long-lost classic 'All For Love'? [Hey A&M, how about an Adams' duets album!] Furthermore, what about all the ballads that they *did* include?

> And '18 Til I Die' – is that a kind of rocker's mid-life crisis? ... Since then, I'd be pleased to say that '18 Til I Die' has grown on me. My problem with the forever young ethos is that it has become a cliché for Mick Jagger and his ilk: lying about your age for profit. Then again, my respect for the mighty-throated Bob Seger – who has matured gracefully on record – dims with every new record facing-up to old age that he releases. The moral here is really that said once too often, anything becomes hollow. Besides, Adams sings the title track like he means it. '18 Til I Die' is a funky anthem, a crank-it-loud personal favourite.

> Perhaps it's time to recognize that we cannot expect the struggling, uneven gems of *Cuts Like A Knife* or the polished hard rock brilliance of *Reckless* ever again, as Adams' career has moved on. What we might hope for instead are songs that balance Bryan's and Mutt Lange's respective song writing talents. The best of all worlds would

be to infuse those with the kind of melodic rock edge that Jim Vallance brought to the proceedings… So much for wishes, but taking '18 Til I Die' as it stands, what we have here is the most autobiographical Adams album in a long while.

On the rock side of the equation, a raw and rootsy mixture bites unwary listeners from the grooves. Left to his own devices, Mutt tends to make songs with chunky chords, chanting vocals, booming production and – yes – big hair. Check out Loverboy's 'Loving Every Minute of It' for a textbook example. Back in June 1996, Bryan told Canada's *Globe and Mail* that *Waking Up The Neighbours* had such a big sound, it was hard to perform live. His consequent effort to avoid the stratospheric, shopping mall production that dogged the last album paid off. Mutt wrote and played on this record, but his arrangements were toned down and placed strategically in the mix, for example in the title track's intro or the verse of '(I Wanna Be Your) Underwear.' Elsewhere the styles vary from the punky throw-away of 'We're Gonna Win' through the slide guitar of 'It Ain't A Party…' (surely the son of 'Can't Stop This Thing We Started'?) to the raucously undulating 'Do To You…' not to mention that catchy scout jingle, 'The Only Thing That Looks Good On Me Is You.' Finally, with its menacing bass line and 1970s feel, 'Black Pearl' stands out as an oddity that will probably sound good as a live track. Meanwhile the rest of the album is peppered with much softer ballads, some of which are collaborations with the formerly-maligned

Michael Kamen. They form a rather odd counterpoint to the rock material. My own favourite is the intimate and relaxing, if rather lengthy, 'Night To Remember.' A while back I thought Adams might be following the Elvis route: releasing ballads as A-sides for his female audience and saving his personal favourite up-tempo numbers for B-sides. It seems, however, that this is more than just marketing, as he seems older and more comfortable with romance.

18 Til I Die might appear a seemingly-incongruous record, but it can be justified as autobiography: Adams wants to sing both rock and ballads too. The diversity of songs on the album is testament to the breadth of black music that Adams has taken on board. He's been listening to John Lee Hooker, Ray Charles, Marvin Gaye and James Brown recently, amongst others. The result is not so much an over-arching album as a collection of songs, and not all of those songs are brilliant. On the other hand, left well alone, Bryan might have slipped into bluesy self-cannibalism and formula music, while Mutt would probably have stuck to his Def Leppard power-house style. *18 Til I Die* holds out the promise that they could consistently write even greater songs as a team next time round. It's a decent mid-career project for a rock'n'roll genius – much better than your average rock album.

Afterword

Continuing with an exploration of Bryan's studio work means assessing his three more recent albums, *On A Day Like Today*, released in 1998, *Room Service* from 2004 and *11* (his eleventh album) from 2008.

While *On A Day Like Today* contained the breezy 'Cloud Number Nine' and the bittersweet but rocking duet with Mel C of The Spice Girls, 'When You're Gone,' it was hampered by a change of record label. A&M sold Adams to Interscope, an operation that started in 1990 and which had gradually broadened its remit from hip-hop to industrial rock and other sounds. Some suggested that the label did not promote Adams' album as they should have done, but the material on it was also not his greatest. Nevertheless, the album went platinum in the UK. One thing that was significant about it was the amount of tracks that Adams co-wrote with the American country-folk artist, Gretchen Peters. Working with a female co-writer evidently added a certain element to the mix, though in this case the tracks co-written with Peters were not the most prominent in the collection.

In 2004, Adams' next album, *Room Service*, was released through Polydor. With Gretchen Peters established as his favourite co-writer, the album did well in Germany, Switzerland and the UK, but sold poorly in the USA, critics claiming that Adams had created a safe but unmemorable recording. Despite this, the Vancouver rocker was still a firm favourite with fans worldwide on the live circuit.

Early in 2006 he became the first artist in the West after the 9/11 attacks to perform in Karachi, Pakistan, at a benefit concert for earthquake victims and underprivileged children. In March 2008, he came back with the next studio album, *11,* and promoted it with an 11 day, 11 country European acoustic tour. For the first time since *Waking Up the Neighbours*, Adams had an album that debuted at number one in his native Canada, but it was much less successful in the American market. Some of the material was classic: take the dramatic single, 'Tonight We Have The Stars,' a co-write between Bryan, Jim Vallance and Gretchen Peters. The song was, in many ways, a return to form. Writing credits on the *11* album shifted significantly towards Bryan's British collaborator, Elliot Kennedy. The Sheffield-based producer has worked with many artists and is credited as a talent developer on the ITV series, X Factor. Adams, in turn, performed on the show late in 2011.

While fans await another studio album, they now have a range of live and greatest hits packages to enjoy. 1988's *Live! Live! Live!*, captured at Belgium's Rock Werchter Festival, was complemented a decade later when Adams' *MTV Unplugged* album was released, followed by *Live at the Budokan* in 2003 and the honest *Bare Bones* collection in 2010. *Bare Bones* went gold in India, a country that Adams recently toured as part of a project to expand his global reach.

In the last two decades of his career Bryan has also overseen several greatest hits packages. After 1993's *So Far So Good* came *The Best of Me*, a compilation designed to punctuate the new millennium and which featured two new songs – the title track and 'Don't Give Up'. Then came *Anthology* in 2005, an extensive two-disc collection from Polydor which mixed a range of studio and live material with occasional remixes. For a limited time the North American pressing came with an additional DVD called *Live In Lisbon*, which was also released as a stand-alone in other territories.

Adams also had several liaisons as a music provider for Hollywood and broadcast television. He re-recorded the Mel C duet 'When You're Gone' in 2005 for the sitcom Stacked. The next year an Adams' penned-and-performed number called 'Never Let Go' appeared at the end of Kevin Costner's film: The

Afterword

Guardian. Next Aretha Franklin and Mary J. Blige performed his tune 'Never Gonna Break My Faith' for the film Bobby and earned Bryan a Golden Globe Nomination. At the end of 2009, a tune performed by Adams called 'You're A Friend of Me' appeared in the Disney film *Old Dogs*, an ensemble comedy that starred Robin Williams and John Travolta.

Larger Hollywood projects have included a gentle soundtrack album for 2002's *Spirit: Stallion of the Cimmaron*, co-written with veteran film score composer Hans Zimmer, and another for 2006's *Colour Me Kubrick* – a film in which John Malkovich played an imposter who pretended to be a famous British film director. 'I'm Not The Man You Think I Am,' from the latter album, saw Adams in Leonard Cohen mode as he accompanied a gentle ballad score.

Beyond Bryan Adams' earlier political ventures – things such as his work for Greenpeace, Live Aid in 1985, The Prince's Trust concerts in 1986 and 1987 and his commemoration of the fall of the Berlin Wall in 1990 – the rocker continued his activism into the 1990s.

In 1993 he joined Farm Aid alongside country veterans Johnny Cash and Willie Nelson. A year later he helped the campaign to officially create a special sanctuary for whales. Eleven years later he joined a CBC benefit concert in Toronto in aid of the Indian Ocean earthquake victims. He also played at Live 8 in Barrie, Ontario and raised millions for Qatar's Reach Out to Asia campaign by doing a benefit concert and auctioning a rare signed guitar. He has been an active campaigner for PETA (People for the Ethical Treatment of Animals) and various children's charities.

While the various albums, singles and political campaigns might have been predicted, what has been more interesting is Bryan's move into photography. Many rock stars collect art as an investment. Some, like Bob Dylan to Paul Stanley of KISS, express their creativity by painting in their spare time. Relatively few vocalists become photographers, however, as they are supposed to be at the centre of the spectacle: in front of the camera, not behind it.

Into the new millennium Bryan was able to leverage his position to become a respected photographer. His photographs have been placed in various fashion and style magazines such as Vogue, Esquire, Harper's Bazaar, i-D, and Interview. He also founded Zoo magazine (not to be confused with the UK lad's mag): an arty, Berlin-based fashion journal.

As a photographer, Adams has had several UK exhibitions, mostly in London, as well as work placed on gallery walls in New York, Paris, Toronto and Montreal. He photographed Queen Elizabeth II during her Golden Jubilee and his shots of her have appeared on postage stamps and in the National Portrait Gallery. He has photographed a wide range of music celebrities from Mick Jagger and Bryan Ferry to Amy Winehouse and Morrissey.

It is strange to think that fans might well bump into Bryan unassumingly carrying a camera. In 2005 a book of his photos was published in the USA by Calvin Klein in aid of breast cancer research under the title of American Women. The Bryan Adams Foundation is a charity that is mainly funded by his photographic income. It aims to support the education of children worldwide.

The new millennium has, then, seen the career of this increasingly mature performer expand across a number of areas. In 2006, Adams was inducted into the Canadian Music Hall of Fame, a strong indication that those struggles of his earlier career were over and that he had been firmly accepted as a national hero. Indeed, in the summer of 2009 Adams was one of a handful of musicians pictured on a series of Canadian postage stamps featuring recording artists. Just before the stamp appeared, the news came that Adams was writing and recording a new album in Paris. In February of the next year, 'One World, One Flame' was released in honour of the Olympics. A German TV station used it as the theme song for coverage of the games in Vancouver. Adams duetted with Nelly Furtado during the opening ceremony from BC Place on a stomping number called 'Bang The Drum'.

The new era sees Bryan Adams, now a father, still writing, still touring – he played Kathmandu in Nepal in 2011 – still campaigning and now taking photos. Speaking of the initial success of *Reckless*, his writing partner Jim Vallance said in 2010: "We couldn't have predicted it. We didn't know it was going to do that well. We just did the best work we could and hoped for the best."[2] But the best was yet to come, and Bryan has clearly achieved it.

[1 & 2] Jason Saulnier interview with Jim Vallance. Available online: http://www.youtube.com/watch?v=I2K7sUJVawc.

We Want The World: Jim Morrison, The Living Theatre and the FBI by Daveth Milton

Jim Morrison was a songwriter, film maker, poet and singer with The Doors. His opponents saw him as a criminal. And more. In an escalating confrontation over the freedom of America, he was up against men who used law to block justice and fear to halt social change. Those men included the FBI's infamous director, J. Edgar Hoover.

Inspired by true events, this imaginative recreation of history re-opens Morrison's secret FBI dossier to reveal his Establishment opponents. Moving between Jim's image, influences and brushes with the law in Phoenix and Miami, Daveth Milton uses meticulous research skills to assess the extent of the conspiracy against the singer. Part meditation, part rock in the dock exposé, We Want The World provides the ultimate account of Jim Morrison's awkward encounter with the Bureau.

Around The World in 80 Scams: An Essential Travel Guide by Peter John

Every year, thousands of people fall victim to various travel scams, crimes and confidence tricks while they travel. Most people escape having simply lost a little money, but many lose much more, and some encounter real personal danger.

Of course, despite the hazards people should not stop travelling - people just need to get smart.

This essential book is a practical, focused, and detailed guide to eighty of the most common scams and crimes travellers might encounter. It is packed with real-world examples drawn from resources across the globe and the author's own travels. Being aware of scammers' tricks is the best way of avoiding them altogether. Forewarned is forearmed.

The Hidden Whisper by Dr JJ Lumsden

pol-ter-geist (noun): 'Noisy spirit'; paranormal source of physical disturbances.

In a retirement community in the desert of southern Arizona, Jack and Chloe Monroe have an unwanted guest. What once appeared merely strange has now taken on sinister overtones. What once seemed a curiosity now seems terrifying.

Paranormal researcher Dr. Luke Jackson reluctantly takes up the investigation and finds himself drawn into a series of unexplained events at the Monroe house. Time is against Luke. He has just one week to unravel the mystery before he must return home.

The Hidden Whisper offers a rare opportunity to enter the intriguing world of the paranormal through the eyes of Luke Jackson. Written by real life parapsychologist Dr. JJ Lumsden, the fictional narrative is combined with extensive endnotes and references that cover Extra Sensory Perception, Psychokinesis, Haunts, Out of Body Experiences and more. A must-read book for anyone who wants to learn about the paranormal.

Graduation: Life Lessons of a Professional Footballer by Richard Lee

The 2010/11 season will go down as a memorable one for Goalkeeper Richard Lee.

After more than ten years at Watford FC, Richard signed for League One outfit Brentford FC, but soon found himself cast aside. Dropped after one game and behind three other goalkeepers before he would get another opportunity - Richard would take on his toughest challenge to date!

Cup wins, penalty saves, hypnotherapy and injury would follow, but these things only tell a small part of the tale.

Suffering from acute mental anxiety throughout his career pushed Richard into making a choice between fight or flight. Could he overcome his fears or take the easy road out and quit? Fortunately for Brentford fans, he chose to fight. Throughout this book, Richard shares his understanding of the mind and how to apply it for high-level performance.

Filled with anecdotes, insights, humour and honesty - Graduation uncovers Richard's campaign to take back the number one spot, save a lot of penalties, and overcome new challenges. What we see is a transformation - beautifully encapsulated in this extraordinary season.